# BLACK WOMEN WRITERS ACROSS CULTURES

# BLACK WOMEN WRITERS ACROSS CULTURES

*An Analysis of Their Contributions*

Edited by

**Valentine Udoh James**
**James S. Etim**
**Melanie Marshall James**
**Ambe J. Njoh**

International Scholars Publications
Lanham • New York • Oxford

PR
9340
.5
.B57
2000

**Copyright © 2000 by**
**International Scholars Publications**

4720 Boston Way
Lanham, Maryland 20706

12 Hid's Copse Rd.
Cumnor Hill, Oxford OX2 9JJ

**Library of Congress Cataloging-in-Publication Data**

Black women writers across cultures : an analysis of their contribution / edited by
Valentine Udoh James...(et al.)
p.   cm.
1.   African literature (English)—Women authors—History and criticism. 2. African
literature (English)—Black authors—History and criticism. 3. American
literature—Afro-American authors—History and criticism. 4. American
literature—Women authors—History and criticism. 5. Women and literature—
United—States—History—20th century. 6. Women and literature—Africa—
History—20th century. 7. Literature, Comparative—African and American. 8.
Literature, Comparative—American and African. 9. Afro-American women in
literature. 10.Women, Black, in literature. I. James, Valentine Udoh, 1952-
PR9340.5.B57  2000     820.9'9287'096—dc21     00—040784 CIP

ISBN 1-57309-415-3 (cloth: alk. ppr)
ISBN 1-57309-416-1 (pbk: alk. ppr.)

⊖™ The paper used in this publication meets the minimum
requirements of American National Standard for Information
Sciences—Permanence of Paper for Printed Library Materials,
ANSI Z39.48—1984

## Dedication

This book is dedicated to our parents.

# Contents

# Preface

*Black Women Writers Across Cultures* is based on a recognition of the practical need to provide more critical materials for upper level undergraduate and beginning graduate students registered in courses devoted entirely to the study of Black women writers of Africa and the Diaspora. This volume was put together largely because we believe that such a book would be readily available for use in teaching courses on Africana women writers and that there is a niche for a book that examines the contributions of Black women writers to their societies. The addition of this volume to the already available literature on Black women writers will increase the breadth of the dialogue on the subject and will highlight some issues that are not discussed adequately. In this book, we therefore seek to provide critical analysis that is both comprehensive and up-to-date on many Africana women writers which beginning students in the field can use as they explore books written by the various writers. Another objective is to bring to the forefront some writers who have not been covered adequately in critical texts. These writers may be less familiar to audiences outside Africa but they, in their own way, have made immense contribution to Africana literature. This book also adds another dimension to the ongoing analysis of the works of such established authors as Flora Nwapa and Bessie Head.

In the last decade or so, many critical works have been published in journals and as books on Black women writers. Since the journal articles are too numerous to cite, a few of the major, critical texts include-Carole B. Davies and Anne Adams Graves "Ngambika: Studies of Women in African Literature" (African World Press, 1986), Adeola James' "In Their Own Words: African

Women Writers' Talk" (Heinemann 1990); Barbara Christian "Black Women Novelists: The Development of a Tradition, 1892-1976" (Greenwood, 1980) and "Black Feminist Criticism: Perspectives on Black Women writers (Pergamon, 1985); Chkwenye Ogunyemi's "African Wo/man Palava: The Nigerian Novel by Women;" Filomina Steady's "The Black Woman Crossculturally" (Schenckman, 1981); Oladele Taiwo's "Female Novelists of Modern Africa" (Heineman, 1984) and Marie Umeh's "Emerging Perspectives on Buchi Emecheta" (AWP, 1996).

Although not exhaustive, the list shows the continuing growth in feminist criticism vis á vis Black women writers. The text *Black Women Writers Across Cultures* continues this direction of providing critical analysis for works of well established as well as less known writers.

Given the ascendancy of feminist criticism, most of the authors in this volume use the feminist/womanist stance in analyzing the works of Black women writers. The book has 11 chapters.

In chapter one, Valentine James, provides a succinct argument for the contribution of Black women writers. This synopsis gives the reader a sense of the reasons why Black women have contributed in important ways to their communities.

In chapter two, Adeola James looks at Bessie Head's works. In Bessie Head's short stories, Adeola James thinks that the reader can see how women are oppressed in both traditional and political systems of colonization.

In chapter three, Adeola's second contribution to this volume, she discusses Zulu Sofola's work. Sofola's works centers on the problems of the Nigerian society as these problems pose stumbling blocks to the advancement of women.

In the fourth chapter, James Etim discusses issues related to feminism as portrayed in the works of Helen Ovbiagele. Here Etim analyses the three young adult novels of the writer, Helen Ovbiagele published in the 1980s showing the feminist consciousness of the principal protagonists.

In chapter five, Francis Ibe Mogu, provides the reader with a powerful essay which reacts to American feminism from an African perspective. The contributor examines the works of Flora Nwapa and Alice Walker in order to accomplish the objective of the chapter.

Chapter six, another of James Etim's contribution examines Flora Nwapa's works in some of the writer's novels and short stories. The discussion focuses on the role and contribution of women in and to society. Nwapa's work was greatly influenced by the society she grew up in.

Chapter seven, "Coramae Richey Mann on Women, Crime, and Color of American Justice" by Joan Mars examines how Mann's enormous literary works have shed light on the impact of the criminal justice process on the lives of minority groups in America.

In chapter eight, the reader revisits Nwapa's works as discussed by Kofi Johnson and Babatunde Oyinade. Here the contributors' chapter focuses on the case study of two of Nwapa's works: *Efuru* and *Idu*. These works depict Nwapa's interpretations of issues of gender, culture, and modernism in Africa.

Chapter nine by Joya Uraizee sheds some light on Buchi Emecheta's interpretation or ideas of political and gender issues in Africa. Emecheta's writings have been examined by many writers who are troubled by the confusion and contradiction that her works present. Uraizee's examination of Emecheta's works seems to echo past reviews of the latter's works.

In chapter ten, Ernest Emenyonu discusses what he thinks is "Flora Nwapa's final legacy." In this chapter, Emenyonu discusses the personal achievement of Nwapa. She was the first woman in Nigeria to accomplish many things such as owning a publishing company. She held many cabinet positions and her writings reflected women's struggles in their African societies.

The eleventh and final chapter in this volume is by Jacquelyn Benton. Benton discusses Grace Nichol's *I is a Long Memoried Woman* and Julie Dash's *Daughters of the Dust: Reversing the Middle Passage*. In this chapter the reader is made aware of the struggles of African, African-American, and Caribbean women's' struggles.

Overall this volume serves as a resource for learning about how Black women writers are interpreting their roles, circumstances and contributions in a global economy.

Valentine Udoh James
James S. Etim
Melanie Marshall James
Ambe J. Njoh

## Acknowledgments

The inspiration for this volume comes from many people and places in Africa and in the Diaspora. The editors of this volume are educators who have been influenced by hundreds of women writers whose works have informed our teaching and writing. Our mothers and sisters remind us of our responsibilities as scholars to be inclusive in all our endeavors and to ensure that debates about Africans and Black women everywhere are informative and articulated properly. We would like to thank our mothers, sisters, and Black women scholars who have influenced our understanding of our complex societies.

# About the Contributors

*The Editors of this Volume*:

**Valentine Udoh James**: Director of African Studies and Associate Professor of Social Science at Kalamazoo College in Michigan. He has authored and edited eleven books and is the recipient of the Fulbright-Hays Faculty Research Abroad Award.

**James S. Etim**: Associate Professor of English in the Department of English and Foreign Languages at Mississippi Valley State University in Itta Bena, Mississippi. He has authored and edited several books and referred articles. He has taught for many years at Nigerian and American Universities.

**Melanie Marshall James**: Senior Research Associate and Creativity Consultant for Inyang International. She provides collaborative services for projects and research on social and educational services. She has worked on numerous international programs, publications, and projects, including hosting a weekly radio call-in talk show.

**Ambe J. Njoh**: Associate Professor in the Public Administration Program at the University of South Florida in St. Petersburg, Florida.

**Jacquelyn Benton**: is a doctoral student in the Department of African American Studies at the University of Wisconsin in Madison.

**Ernest N. Emenyonu**: Visiting Professor of the African and African-American Studies Department at Brandeis University. He has authored and co-edited several books on African Literature. Until recently, he was Deputy Vice Chancellor at the University of Calabar in Nigeria.

**Adeola James**: Senior Lecturer and Head of Department of English at the University of Guyana. Her most recent book is *In Their Own Voices: African Women Writers Talk* (Heinemann, 1990).

**Kofi Johnson**: Associate Professor of Political Science at North Carolina Central University. He is a Ghanian native with extensive field experience in Africa.

**Joan Mars**: Assistant Professor of Public Affairs in the Department of Public Affairs at the University of Wisconsin in Oshkosh.

**Francis Ibe Mogu**: is a Senior Lecturer in the Department of English at the University of Lagos in Akoka-Lagos, Nigeria.

**Babatunde Oyinade**: Assistant Professor of Communications at Shaw University. Publications have appeared in edited volumes dealing with issues of governance and sustainable development.

**Joya Uraizee**: Assistant Professor of English in the Department of English at Saint Louis University in Missouri.

# CHAPTER ONE

## The Keys to the Contribution of Black Women Writers: A Synopsis
## Valentine Udoh James

Every African man of substance knows that he owes his success to a strong African woman (mother) who inculcated in him the burning desire to strive to succeed, the ability to be tenacious and persevere in the presence of many obstacles. These women, whether they are urbanites or rural settlers know that raising their children by teaching them the norms of society, acceptable etiquette, and the importance of extended family systems will be beneficial to preserving the African culture. The position of women, regardless of the status one assigns them, does not impede women from clinging onto their most central duty which is to ensure and safeguard the family through the education of the children. African boys and girls received this attention from their mothers but in different ways.

Black women in the Diaspora have been the anchor of their families and home. In many instances when societal policies have made it impossible for men to remain within the home or other pressures have made it impossible for fathers to be available for their children, the women have taken charge and have done exceptionally well in being heads of households.

One of the African oral traditions, storytelling, has persevered over the years and helps to inform the young people of Africa. In the United States and other areas of the Diaspora, the tradition of storytelling is slowly garnering steam in many educational and ceremonial circles. Oral story telling is gaining recognition and resurgence and can be witnessed in many places outside of Africa. Black women are playing significant roles in this effort as they have done throughout history.

I have a very vivid memory of the story telling period. I grew up in a family of seven (five males and two females) and I remember very well when every night we would gather at my mother's feet to listen to the bed time stories that were told completely by heart. We had our favorites and it did not matter how many times we heard them, they always left indelible impressions on us. The stories  portrayed courage, dedication, and morality. Although women like my mother had little formal education, they told the stories that informed and educated us. The stories are embedded in African cultures.

There is a new breed of women story-tellers today. They are powerful and energetic women and the messages of their stories come to us in the printed form. These women writers, like those who could not write (my mother being one) tell a story about the world they live in. The one that denies women a complete voice in spite of women's contribution to the building of the societies in which they live. They address political, economic, social, environmental, and scientific issues. Their writings question colonial and post colonial institutions' impact on women's status in Africa and posit new paradigms for a better and more equitable society.

Black women scholars are reshaping the context of academic and policy engagement and are challenging the past notions of development and governance. For instance Kalu (1996:21) states that many African women scholars and writers are beginning to pose questions about the relevance of literary work on sustainable development. She notes in discussing the relationship between African literature and sustainable development: "What, then, does African literature have to do with sustainable African development and African women?"

The answer to this question should be put in the context of examining African societies and how they function in pre-colonial times, colonial times, and post colonial times. Kalu (1996:275) notes that "most pre-colonial African people had thought through most of the issues and problems of their existence and were prepared by traditional wisdom to take charge of the world." There is no question that women played an important role during this period and still do because of women's influence in agriculture and raising the family.

Black women writers' contributions to their societies and the global communities are many and varied and the contributions mirror the complexities, experiences, struggles, and circumstances that women confront in their different environments. No matter what the differences may be, there are striking similarities which seem to connect these writers. Generalizations about Black women writers can be made in terms of contemporary critical theory, culture, and politics. Although the variety of linguistic landscape, colonial and post colonial experiences present some degree of problems, one can assess the significance and value of the writings. They all tell stories about African circumstances and provide a dialogue for informing, educating and building better and stronger institutions necessary to expose the circumstances that need to be changed.

Black women writers, especially those in Africa, do their writing under difficult circumstances. The dire economic, social, and political conditions in some countries have added to the difficult circumstances under which they work. This point was made very vividly in Charlotte Bruner's (1983) edited work: *Unwinding Threads: Writing by Women in Africa* in which she examined the writings of women in western, eastern, southern, and northern Africa. In her preface she noted that an African woman writer must be a maverick in defying the traditional roles of motherhood and wife and stepping into an individualistic mode of operating in the society instead of the collective. Bruner (1983:xv) notes:

> The African woman writing fiction today has to be somehow exceptional. Despite vast differences in traditions and beliefs among African societies, any female writer must have defied prevailing tradition if she speaks out as an individual and as a woman. In order to reach an international audience directly, she often has had to cross linguistic barriers. She may well have confronted the dictates of societies in which the perpetuation of a tradition submerges the contribution of the innovator, in which the subservience of the individual to the community is

> reinforced by group sanctions. In such societies, the
> accepted role of any artist is to commemorate
> custom, in words, in song, and in the selection of
> the details that validate the accepted ethics of that
> society. Generally, then, the perpetuator is preferred
> to the creator. To be outstanding is to court
> rejection.

The African women writers examined in this volume have contributed to the improvement of their societies, the education of their people, the elevation of the status of women, and are recognized outside of their own cultures. They have paid a price for this appreciation but the uplifting of their communities is probably worth such a sacrifice.

In recent times, we have seen scholars examine the political and social contributions of literary works of writers. Subbarao's (1993) examination of Nadine Gordimer's contribution to South Africa's political scene is worth noting. Gordimer played an important role in making her work reflect South Africa's problems of Apartheid. This gave the global community a glimpse into what the Black life was like under the oppressive regime. The social responsibility of writers is probably more significant than their responsibility to the creative craft (that is speaking from the collective benefit perspective). The literature on the social significance of Black women writings has not received enough attention.

Black women everywhere experience problems set forth by patriarchal societies that are exacerbated by problems of modernization and how to manage contemporary problems of relationships. This difficult landscape through which women must negotiate is vividly documented in essays, stories, poems, and interviews with Black women living in the Diaspora (Great Britain) in Grewal et al. (1988) work—*Charting the Journey: Writings by Black and Third World Women.* In one of the essays titled "Gal-You Come from Foreign," Claudette Williams discusses the trials and tribulations of Black women in Britain. She is frustrated by the dominant white society-a culture different from her Jamaican roots. She identifies world events which help shape her Black and cultural identity and the impacts of the written words about Blacks and by Blacks that helped in clarifying doubts she had. She writes:

> Black consciousness enabled me to make the connection between class and racism, and offered the context within which to understand migration from the Caribbean in the numbers and at that particular historical time: why we acquire the worst housing, education and health care, why we are targeted for racial abuse and assaults. We learned that racism and economic exploitation are features of capitalism and necessary for the advancement of British capitalism. However, with political enlightenment came contradictions that became very antagonistic with women's demands for autonomous groups (p. 155).

Many writings by Black women discuss how to cope with societal problems. Women in Black families are the ones who experience the most difficulties especially as they are the ones who have to deal with raising the children and addressing the immediate concerns of the family. They cope with these societal problems in different ways. In her essay "I am a Black Women" in *Charting the Journey: Writing by Black and Third World Women*, Olivette Cole-Wilson (1988:162) notes:

> subsequently, I joined a Black women's consciousness raising group, attended the Organization of Women of Asian and African Descent (OWAD) conferences and generally made more positive connections with Black women. As my involvement with the Black feminist movement in Britain has grown I have begun to appreciate and gain strength from many of the women I have met or known of in Sierra Leone. When I am told here in England that feminism is a "white women's thing" I can cite examples of women who have been fighting for centuries to be treated as people in their own right.

Many fiction and non-fiction books written by African women have not received the attention that they deserve. Ogunyemi (1996:1) in her introduction of her book *Africa Wo/man and Palava: The Nigerian Novel by Women* laments:

> ... African women go unseen, unheard, and unheeded, since novels written by them and about them are still generally ignored by readers and critics. Nevertheless, the women novelists writing for an adult audience are numerous and insightful.

The success of African male writers has forced the global and African communities to pay attention to those well-known male writers and as such the uniqueness and the critical significance of African women/Black women writers is ignored. Ogunyemi's work clearly presents some of the intricate and complicated ways in which African women's writings have complemented and filled in the gaps in the African men's writings. The women's writings have a vivid points of departure and certainly an authenticity which reflect the history, the culture, and the conditions under which they do their writing. The evolution of development processes in Africa have played major roles in the handicapping of African women writers. Theirs has been a journey of great struggle and adaptation. The educational processes have not been favorable in order to allow a much larger number of talented young African girls to aspire to become professionals. Those who have succeeded are from the elite families but still bear the burden of having to succumb to societal standards of being wives and mothers.

The courage and triumph of the women writers that are examined in this volume have historical context-from the colonial period to the contemporary world. The viewpoints are influenced by European, African, African-American and feminists debates. One must understand that African/Black women writings incorporate a sense of community. These women write to show how the suffering and pain of men and children is their suffering. The African writer's care for humanity, people, and society is best put in the description of Bessie Head's work:

> I can attest to the fact that her personal struggle was

> indeed very real, but it never defeated her belief in people. Her work stands as a testament to the hope for a better world, and the drive to write under great adversity was one to which she completely dedicated her life until its end. About this achievement it seems appropriate to remember the words spoken over one of the most enduring of Shakespeare's tragic idealists: "And flights of angels sing thee to thy rest" (Daniel Gover cited in A. V. Sulu p. 246).

Many of the writings of Black women reflect the societal relationships that are breaking down and these writings portray the causes of community problems. Modern African societies are plagued by numerous problems of economy, politics, and general instability. Many of the writings reflect these conditions and because African societies are undergoing significant changes, African women writers do not enjoy the stability that is crucial in making them truly successful in a global context. Sometimes non-Africans who examine African women writers misunderstand the limitations imposed by society on African women writers. These critics claim that African women writers are unable to become"ideal writers" who respect and understand a global perspective of writing because of their own inability to transcend their immediate surroundings.

Rani (1994:196) argues that there is confusion in some of Flora Nwapa's writings. He submits:

> She therefore exaggerates certain minor points more or less bringing her situations down to low comedy. There is at times a genuine doubt whether she is writing only for the native audience or for the readers outside Africa. So when it comes to the point of describing a scene which is unfamiliar to people outside Africa she uses the method of giving minute, detailed descriptions and explanation in order to justify her stand.

Flora Nwapa's descriptions of scenes, one could argue, is a genuine attempt to accommodate all linguistic groups within Nigeria and for that matter within

Africa. It is also true that every writer communicates from a cultural background which begins with one's basic and primary language. It is not uncommon to see in African writings a long and extended description of scenes which by the way, is meant to add color, aesthetics, and drama to the situations. It is not a problem of language as Rani assessment may seem to suggest rather it is a cultural style.

I would like to embellish this point by examining the following discussion in "the Road to Benin" an essay from Nwapa's *This is Lagos and Other Stories* (1971:30):

> Her husband was a daily paid labourer. For years,
> he was daily paid. That meant that when he was ill,
> he was not paid.

Nwapa used the second and third sentences to make her audience understand what it means to be daily paid. An American audience is more familiar with one being an "hourly employed person;" which means that one uses a time sheet to record time one spends on a job on a daily basis. It would not be fair to claim that Nwapa's writings are handicapped by language but that she recognizes local colloquial expressions and attempts to remedy the situation through explanations.

Another point that must be emphasized about most Black women writers is the desire to make society recognize the significance of women's contribution and for those in position of authority to foster the inclusion of women in decision making arenas. Clearly Nwapa's works attempted to make this point. In works such as: *This is Lagos and other Stories, Women are Different*, and *One is Enough*, Nwapa certainly gets the point across about the need for African women to be strong and financially independent and their capacity to take care of themselves-especially urban women.

It should be pointed out that Black women writers have contributed significantly to the debate of development by addressing the many deplorable conditions under which women perform their "duties" and by so doing calling local, national, and international attention to the plight of women. Global efforts to address the problems women are gaining ground and many policies are being institutionalized to remedy the conditions.

## REFERENCES

Bruner, H. Charlotte (ed). 1983. *Unwinding Threads: Writing by Women in Africa*. London: Heinemann.

Cole-Wilson, Olivette. 1988. "I am a Black Woman" in Shabnam Grewal and Pratibha Parmar (eds.). *Charting the Journey: Writings by Black and Third World Women*. London: Sheba Feminist Publishers.

Grewal, Shabnam; Jackie Kay; Liliane Landor, Gail Lewis, and Pratibha Parmar (eds.). 1988. *Charting the Journey: Writings by Black and Third World Women*. London: Sheba Feminist Publishers.

Kalu, C. Anthonia. 1996. "Women and the Social Construction of Gender in African Development." *Africa Today*. Volume 43 Number 3 July/Sept.

Nwapa, Flora. 1986. *Women are Different*. Enugu, Nigeria: Tana Press Ltd.

_____. 1981. *One is Enough*. Enugu, Nigeria: Tana Press.

_____. 1971. *This is Lagos and Other Stories*. Enugu, Nigeria: Nwankwo-Ifejika and Co. Publishers Ltd.

Ogunyemi, Okonjo Chikwenye. 1996. *Africa Wo/man Palava. The Nigerian Novel by Women*. Chicago: TheUniversity of Chicago Press.

Rani, K. Nirupa. 1994. "The Feminine Perspective: A Study of Flora Nwapa's Efuru and Idu" in R. K. Dhawan(ed.) *African Literature*. New Delhi India: Prestige Books.

Rao, A. Ramakrishna and C. R. Visweswara Rao (eds.). 1993. *Indian Response to African Writing*. New Delhi,India: Prestige.

Subbarao, C. 1993. "The Writer's Conscience: A Reading of Nadine Gordimer's *The Essential Gesture*" in Ramakrishna Rao and Visweswara Rao (eds.). *Indian Response to African Writing*. New Delhi, India:Prestige Books.

Sulu, A. V. 1994. "Bessie Head: A Literary Profile" in R. K. Dhawan (ed.) *African Literature*. New Delhi, India:Prestige Books.

William, Claudette. 1988. "Gal ... You Come from Foreign" in Shabnam Grewal and Pratibha Parmar (eds.). *Charting the Journey: Writings by Black and Third World Women*. London: Sheba Feminist Publishers.

# CHAPTER TWO

## Bessie Head's Perspectives on Women
### Adeola James

## BACKGROUND

Bessie Head, who died prematurely in 1986 at the age of forty-eight years, is recognized today as one of Africa's leading writers. At the time of her death she had published three novels, a collection of short stories, a book based on oral traditions, and an historical book[1] Since her death, there have been further evidence of her fecund mind; another collection of short stories, a selection of her letters, and a full biography have been published.[2] There are researches being done all over the world which will, eventually appraise us of the full stature of this dedicated, but enigmatic mind.

In studying Head's works, one thing that is most striking is her concern about the position of women under an oppressed traditional as well as the political system of colonization. The colonial period, though gave power to the Africans, the experience of women did not change much. Head, in giving voice to the experiences of women, invokes a feminist criticism of her work, though she herself might have resisted this definition. Her objection, like that of many even today, would derive from the incorrect negativism attached to the term "feminist." A clear definition of my premise will make my purpose clear.

> Feminists [are those who] believe that women have been locked off in a condition of lesser reality by the dominant attitudes and customs of our culture. We find these attitudes and customs reified in the institutions of literature and literary criticism.[3]

From the above definition we can understand that feminist criticism can be described as a mode of negation seen within a fundamental dialectic. The fundamental dialectic being the radical transformation of consciousness taking place at this time in history, almost everywhere in the world including Africa. What is generally referred to as "the women question" is the recognition of the necessity of restoring women to their place in history, recognizing that they have always been around though, ignored and denied voice. The feminist approach, when applied to the critique of Head's works, yields a rewarding result as I intend to prove in this chapter.

Chinua Achebe is one of the earliest writers in post-colonial Africa to give voice to the exploitation of Africa through colonialism and the ensuing tragic results of that experience. Indeed most of the first generation writers like Soyinka, Okot p. Bitek, Ngugi wa Thiong'o, Okigbo and J. P. Clark, to name a few, attained renown through their powerful dramatization of the inescapable conflicts within African societies following the colonial encounter.

Literature should enlarge one's vision of life but for the first two decades of writing in Africa, literature has neglected the representation of men and women. Women were made invisible and voiceless or, at best, they were presented in stereotypical images. Women writers reversed the invisibility and voicelessness of women in literature and, in a general way, fought against the culture of silence in which African women were traditionally drowned. Most importantly, through their writing we begin to understand women's position on important issues about the African world view, history, politics, heritage, the Diaspora, love, bonding, and relationship.

The fundamental contribution of the African women writers is the location of the conflicts and the ultimate tragedy of Africa in the exploitation and deprivation of her women folk by men folk. Bessie Head, Ama Ata Aidoo, Buchi Emecheta, and Zulu Sofola have written boldly about this in the hope that they can add their voices to the recipe for change. Women writers have dramatized the double burden of their women folk. They are oppressed and exploited by the inhuman exertions of the twin mode of capitalism and colonialism. Underlying this, however, is the position of weakness to which women are traditionally relegated. Bessie Head clearly and unequivocally states:

> The ancestors made so many errors and one of the most bitter-making things was that they relegated to men a superior position in the tribe, while women were regarded, in a congenital sense, as being an inferior form of human life. To this day women still suffer from all the calamities that befall an inferior form of life (p.92).[4]

The personal is the political. The women writers have brought the female world into the public view in a way that men either have deliberately or inadvertently failed to do. Our women writers represent female experience from the woman's perspective and create complex and credible images of women as they come to terms with their lives as modern women in a continent that has been traumatized by slavery and colonialism, but is undergoing promising transformation.

## SUMMARY

> Long ago, when the land was only cattle tracks and footpaths, the people lived together like a deep river. which was unruffled by conflict ... (p. 1).[5]
>      What could be done? Nothing could sort out the world. It would always be a painful muddle (p. 109).[6]

These quotations are the opening and closing statements found in *The Collector of Treasures*. In a way they sum up the history of Africa, capturing succinctly what has happened to us over these last few centuries, the transformation from an "unruffled" life to "a painful muddle." Head's mature vision and painful personal experiences enabled her to analyze what is our tragedy. I believe she succeeds in taking us beyond the great statement of this tragedy dramatized in *Things Fall Apart*. Head takes us beyond colonial injustices, locating the problem of Africa in the sufferings and injustices endured by her women throughout the ages.

The first statement is from a story which celebrates the great love between two young people. Sebembele was willing to renounce his kingdom for the sake of a woman who loved him. It was acknowledged by all that Rankana was "a beautiful woman ...she was gentle and kind and loving..." When Sebembele refused to bow to the machinations of his brothers and stood firmly by Rankana and his son, he won the respect of his people who "saw that they had a ruler who talked with deeds rather than words" (p. 5).

The second statement above is Thato's observation on the incredible muddle people make of their lives each day: she has just finished briefing her husband on happenings in the village and what a list of woes!

> There's trouble again between Felicia and her husband ... Rapula had taken up with a she been queen and arrived home dead drunk every other night and beat his wife because she complained and scolded ....

Reddock defines feminism as

> the awareness of the oppression, exploitation and/or subordination of women within society and the conscious action to change and transform this situation.

Head was interested in changing the oppressive situation of women as she observed and experienced it in Africa. Before she could do this, her first step was to make us aware of the exploitation and subordination of the women. Hence, life for women, in all its ramifications, is her primary theme. Her analysis in novel after is detailed, clear and incisive as we will observe as I examine each work.

## THE TRAGEDY OF MALE EGO

"The Collector of Treasures," appropriately, the story that gives that collection of short stories its title, contains the most moving portraiture of a tragic, dignified, and most admirable woman. In analyzing her fate, the narrator gives us the most profound analysis of the tragedy of the African man, from which that of the woman cannot be divorced. As a central statement in Head's writing, one which is germane to the perspectives she presents on women, it deserves to be quoted in full. The author-narrator asserts that "there were really only two kinds of men in the society. The one kind created such misery and chaos that he could be broadly damned as evil." Having likened his behaviour to that of "the village dogs chasing a bitch on heat" describing graphically the repulsive excesses of the winner, she says "like the dogs and bulls and donkeys, he also accepted no responsibility for the young he procreated and like the dogs and bulls and donkeys, he also made females abort." She continues, "since that kind of man was in the majority in the society" and since, "he was responsible for the complete breakdown of family life," he could be analyzed over three time spans. What follows is a most gripping analysis of the tragic destruction of the African male ego, his attempt to recapture his sense of manliness by subjugating his female counterpart. This results in the chaos that we are familiar with. In explaining the present situation, Head takes us through the history of Africa seen in three different eras-the time of the ancestors, the colonial period and independence. She writes,

> In the old days, before the colonial invasion of Africa, he was a man who lived by the traditions and taboos outlined for all the people by the forefathers of the tribe. He had little individual freedom to assess whether these traditions were compassionate or not-they demanded that he comply and obey the rules, without thought. But when the laws of the ancestors are examined, they appear on the whole to have been vast, external disciplines for the good of the society as a whole with little attention given to individual preferences and needs."

Of course, the rules of the ancestors are not faultless and one of the major errors they made is "that they relegated to men a superior position in the tribe, while women were regarded, in a congenital sense, as being an inferior form of human life."

The male ego was further destroyed in the colonial era, the period of migratory mining labour. Worse still, this form of labour destroyed family life— "it broke the old, traditional form of family life and for long periods a man was separated from his wife and children while he worked for a pittance in another land in order to raise the money to pay British Colonial polltax." The African man lost his self respect because he became "the boy of the white man."

Independence brought very little relief to his pain and the destiny of his people. Head writes:

> African independence seemed merely one more affliction on top of the afflictions that had visited this man's life.

The thrust of Head's penetrating analysis is to seek the meaning of our history while showing how women have survived the massive onslaught on their beings. Whether it was during the time of the ancestors, the colonial period, or the independence period the male whose sense of Self-worth has been destroyed always "turns to the woman in a dizzy kind of death dance of wild destruction and dissipartion." As a result of this exploration Head's fictional world is peopled by women who have not only survived but have assisted the regeneration of their menfolk, paving the way for a new harmonious existence.

## THE SEARCH FOR SPIRITUAL AND PHYSICAL EMANCIPATION

*When Rain Clouds Gather* dramatizes emancipatory yearnings, the search for both physical and spiritual emancipation. For Makhaya, who leaves his mother in South Africa "in a state of complete collapse" to travel somewhere because "he could not marry and have children in a country, where Black men were called 'boy' and 'kaffir,' his search for liberation from political oppression is actively connected with greater spiritual enlightenment which he experiences in the course of his moral development living and working in Botswana. Another male, Gilbert, and Englishman, disengages himself from the country of 'nice, orderly queues' where everybody lines up for a place and position in the world (p. 28)." Like Makhaya, he is in search of fulfillment and a more meaningful existence. In the village of Golema Mmidi where he devotes himself to assisting 'in agricultural development and improved techniques of food production,' he finds a richer life. Both Makhaya's and Gibert's moral and spiritual development are linked with the lives of three women who become the focus of our attention in the novel, namely Mma-Millipede, Maria, and Pauline.

Mma-Millipede is the mother of the village, she recalls the West Indian mother (the mainstay of family life since slavery), and the traditional African grandmother who used to regulate the affairs of everyone. Mma-Millipede is described as "one of those rare individuals with a distinct personality at birth ... she was able to grasp the religion of the missionaries and use its message to adorn and enrich her own originality of thought and expand the natural kindness of her heart (p. 63)." When Dinorego becomes acquainted with Makhaya's problems, the old man advises the younger one "you must approach my friend Mma-Millipede ... she may help you to find the woman you seek, as she knows the heart of everyone (p.91)." The unintrusive voice of the narrator makes an important observation about Mma-Millipede. She

> had traced two distinct relationships women had with men in her country. The one was a purely physical relationship. It caused no mental breakdown and was free and casual each woman having six' or seven lovers, including a husband as well. The other was more serious and more rare. It could lead to mental breakdown and suicide on the part of the woman.'[7]

She prefers the other one, reasoning that

> it was far better to have a country of promiscuous
> women than a country of dead women (p.91-2).

With such a pragmatic attitude she looks after the interest of all who come within her orbit of activities. She senses Maria's interest better than her father and through her intervention both Gilbert and Maria are able to achieve fulfillment.

Similarly, she guides Makhaya through bitterness, hatred, and despair to accept all men as his brothers. He observes that "the old woman had a fire inside her that radiated outward and he could feel it and it warmed him. ... He liked this direct people-caring and this warm fire in an old woman (p. 121)." In this enriching exchange, Makhaya begins to assume "new mental outlooks." Once he is spiritually opened up he is able to say to Paulina "perhaps, I'll find out what love is as we go along together (p. 147)." His voyage towards self-discovery, personal and spiritual regeneration, is complete in his union with Paulina and he observes:

> All his life he had wanted some kind of Utopia, and
> he had rejected in his mind and heart a world full of
> ailments and faults. He had run and run away from
> it all ... loving one woman had brought him to this
> realization: that it was only people who could bring
> the real rewards of living: that it was only people
> who give love and happiness (p. 152).[8]

Gilbert's life is less agonizing because of his belonging to a race that is on the giving end of oppression and therefore, immuned to it. Nevertheless, if he were to experience the new dispensation of spiritual awakening he too had to leave his accustomed comfort. For when life is too selfishly smooth, it could kill with its boredom and monotony. Mma-Millipede adores Gilbert "as she identified him with her own love of mankind."

It is Mma-Millipede's task to direct the young to develop a creative attitude that nurtures life. She does this with a loving heart and genuine generosity.

Maria is regarded by her father as "a difficult daughter." Old Dinorego had led Makhaya into the village in the hope that he might prove to be a suitable suitor for his daughter.

Maria appears in the novel on very few occasions. She is of significance only in relation to the fulfilling relationship that emerges between herself and Gilbert. Through his friend Makhaya, Gilbert affirms that life might have something more to offer than "running away from it." He confesses that ninety per cent of the time he doesn't want a woman. "Then also there's that ten percent when I'm lonely, but I don't know of any woman who'd go for the ten percent. (p. 29)." Maria "was one of those women who had a life of her own" she is "a preoccupied self-absorbed woman," with "an almighty air of neatness and orderliness about her ... her small black eyes never seemed to gaze outward, but inward." She is a woman of few words. Such a woman is able to transform "the ten percent" of life that a very busy man like Gilbert could share her. Maria is presented as the typical housewife who is industrious. Apart from keeping her home she joins in the agricultural projects organized by her husband and Makhaya. She discharges her responsibility towards her community; at the cattle post, she takes on the responsibility of cooking for the men, and for Paulina's household as well. Her reaction on the occasion of the tragic death of Paulina's son is the only positive one. She observes:

> ... death was like trying to clutch the air, and you had to let it be and slowly let it pass aside, without fuss and indignity. Instead, you had to concentrate the mind on all that was still alive and treat it as the most precious treasure you had ever been given (p.153).

She is a woman of action rather than words. Her affirmation of life is contained in her reply to her husband who informs her during the terrible drought that "even the trees were dying, from the roots upwards." Maria said

> No, you may see no rivers on the ground but we
> keep the rivers inside us. That is why all good
> things and all good people are called rain.
> Sometimes we see the rain clouds gather even
> though not a cloud appears in the sky. It is all in our
> heart (p.157.)

Maria encapsulates women's spiritual strength and deep hope that life will last in spite of temporary setbacks.

Paulina bridges the age gap between Mma-Millipede and Maria and forms the last in Head's images of well-grounded women, portrayed with positive and life-enhancing spirits. Paulina is industrious, in addition "she was daring and different" which make all the other women follow her leadership. What sets her apart most significantly is her ability to think and analyze. Paulina, unlike the other women has no permanent lover or husband. The women come to admit that the reason why Paulina dominated them all was because she was the kind of woman who could not lie to men (p. 86). She fears "the untrustworthiness of men with no strength or moral values." Intuitively she feels something is wrong with a whole society which "had connived at producing a race of degenerate men by stressing their superiority in the law and overlooking how it affected them as individuals (p.86)."

Paulina, the narrator says:

> Was not like the women of Golema Mmidi,
> although she had been born into their kind of world
> and fed on the same diet of their maize porridge by
> a meek, repressed, dull-eyed mother (p.18).

She is distinguished by a superior education and by retaining since childhood a "fresh, lively curiosity." What we remember most about this dignified woman is her natural ability to lead. Gilbert's request that she should get one hundred women organized into a tobacco-growing co-operative receives a "generous smile from her. Later it is largely through her effort that this project, which transformed the lives of the village women who have never worked for money, succeeded.

What are most memorable about her are her controlled and courageous stance in time of tragedy, when her son dies alone at the cattlepost; most importantly, her ability to question radically old and popularly accepted practices in the man/woman relationship.

She was aware of her physical need but she would not yield to having lovers because of a "blind and intense desire to own and possess a man to herself. "But in a society like this" she asks "which man cared to be owned and possessed when there were so many women freely available?" She objected to "the excessive love-making" which was purposeless and aimless, "just like tipping everything into an awful cess-pit where no one really cared to take a second look. Paulina "was too proud a woman to be treated like a "cess-pit" she wanted "a man who wasn't a free for-all."

Following this line of thoughts to its conclusion she adds,

> No doubt, the other women longed for this too because intense bloody battles often raged between women and women over men, and yet, perversely, they always set themselves up for sale to the first bidder who already had so many different materials in his shop that he was simple bored to death by the display (p. 104).
>
> Botswana men no longer cared. In fact a love affair resulting in pregnancy was one sure way of driving a man away and it was a country of fatherless children now (p. 111).

Wisdom then lies in self control and certain understanding among the women to prevent the exploitation the men are permitted because of their weakness and disunity.

Paulina's concern is not for herself alone. Her own experience enables her to empathize with the suffering of women in a society in which

> Every protection for women was breaking down and being replaced by nothing. And there was something so deeply wrong in the way a woman had to live, holding herself together with her

backbone, because, no matter to which side a
woman might turn, there was this trap of loneliness.
Most women had come to take it for granted,
entertaining themselves with casual lovers. Most
women with fatherless children thought nothing of
sending a small boy out to a lonely cattle post to
herd cattle to add to the family income. But then,
such women expected life to give them nothing.
And if you felt the strain of such a life, all the way
down your spine surely it meant that you were just
holding on until such time as a miracle occurred?
And how many miracles an ordinary woman needed
these days. Paulina sighed bitterly and deeply ... (p.
111).

In the creation of Paulina, Head presents one of her most touching and
profoundest characters. The circumstances of her life, her inter-relationships with
others, are real ones that any reader can identify with, so compelling and truthful
are they. In her creation, Head further shows that feminism is not a creation of the
misguided western-educated African woman. You don't have to read too much to
learn where your shoes are hurting.

There are certain areas of Paulina's attitude that need changing as well.
She forbids Makhaya to help her in preparing the meal saying "Don't touch the
fire. 'It 's woman's work'." Most African men and women will agree with this
sentiment. However, in their journey together towards enlightenment Makhaya
teaches Paulina the new way. He says to her, "It's time you learned that men live
on this earth too. If I want to make tea, I'll make it, and if I want to sweep the
floor, I'll sweep it (p. 130)."

Makhaya was thankful for Paulina's love which "was like a warm sun on
all the shadows of his life." At the same time he notes that "a woman's life was a
clutter of small everyday things-of babies, gossip, pots, food, fires, cups, and
plates (p. 142)." Is Makhaya suggesting that the African woman too deserves a
better life? The love that developed between Paulina and Makhaya gives the
reader an opportunity to see an enlightened, symbiotic relationship in action. At

the end Makhaya is able to affirm that "loving one woman had brought him to this realization, that it was only people who could bring the real rewards of living, that it was only people who give love and happiness (p. 152)."

Paulina is Head's presentation of ideal womanhood, the maturing influence of suffering and an unflagging ability to look life straight in the face without giving up the struggle to change it.

In the presentation of these three female characters-Mma-Millipede, Maria, and Paulina-Head portrays women as life-givers, life-preservers and life-transformers. The authorial voice paying homage to the women for transforming village-life by their work in the tobacco cooperative comments,

> No men ever worked harder than Botswana women, for the whole burden of providing food for big families rested with them. It was their sticks that threshed the corn at harvesting time and their winnowing baskets that filled the air for miles and miles around with the dust of husks, and they often, in addition to broadcasting the seed when the early rains fell, took over the tasks of the men and also ploughed the land with oxen (p.97).

Their successful elimination of the retrograde chief Matenge "a Solomon stalking the land in his golden Chevrolet" (p. 173) is an indication of the miracle that could happen when women are united. In a male-dominated world, Head is pointing to the channels of change.


## MARU


In *Maru*, her second novel, Head presents a woman's version of racial problem in Africa. She tells an interviewer that "*Maru* was a thesis against racialism .... It is an examination of racial prejudices but I used black against black instead of white against black." The novel describes the experience of a Masarwa, an untouchable who was found and raised by a white missionary. In dramatizing this story, Head exposes the senseless prejudices that separate us. Though Head's stated focus is on racial prejudice, the novel offers some clear perspectives on the position of women in Africa. Women are the sufferers but in their suffering they find the grace to become the agent of change. Margaret, the protagonist, highlights this in her own statement when she remarks "There was no word to explain the torture of those days, but out of it she had learned" (p. 102).[9] The woman may be a victim of prejudice, yet it is through her positive attitude that she leads her people through the process of reexamination and ultimate change. This meaning is enclosed in Margaret's painting. Commenting on Margaret's work, in one of the central passages of the book, Maru remarks:

> She chose her themes from the ordinary, common happenings in the village as though those themes were the best expression of her own vitality. The women carried water buckets up and down the hill but the eye was thrown, almost by force, towards the powerful curve of a leg muscle, *resilience* in the back and neck, and the *animated* expressions and gestures of the water-carriers as they stopped to gossip .... Look! Don't you see! We are the people who have the strength to build a new world! (p. 107-108). [Italics are supplied.]

This is not Maru's voice *per se*, but that of the omniscient narrator paying tribute to the African woman as she emerges through suffering, endurance and struggle into the dawn of a new world.

## A QUESTION OF POWER

It is Head's conviction that the new world cannot be created without excruciating suffering. This is the conviction dramatized in *A Question of Power*, the most powerful of Head's writing at the same time the most enigmatic. *A Question of Power*, is Head's version of "life-writing in the feminine," where her protagonist, Elizabeth struggles to define herself as a subject through figuring out her life story in different versions. It is in this novel that we encounter Head's most sustained effort to put the African experience in the context of her own world view. She writes:

> In my novel, *A Question of Power*, I was extremely
> bothered to define evil. I was looking for answers
> all along to questions of exploitation. And I was
> looking for balances; that is, if we have to live with
> good and evil we ought to present them as they
> really are.[10]

It is not without significance that Head focuses her exploration of evil on the life of one woman. It is through Elizabeth that the fundamental question of exploitation and suffering is fleshed out. Head combines the physical with the psychic in dramatizing through Elizabeth's life, the Biblical verse "For we wrestle not against flesh and blood, but against principalities, against powers, against the rulers of the darkness of this world, against spiritual wickedness in high places" (Ephesians 6:12). In this statement, Paul might have been directing his warnings at men; in Head's view, however, it seems that women, particularly Black women, are the ones who face this devastating apocalyptic struggle.

There are four unforgettable women in *A Question of Power*, Elizabeth, Kenosi, Birgette, and Camilla. All four serve as counterpoints to one another revealing the author's views on the experiences of women.

It is Elizabeth's story for we encounter the other characters in relation to her need of them or in her reaction to them. The plot of the novel is the evolution of Elizabeth's soul. This is gathered from the opening paragraphs of the book. Sello wonders

> how often was a learner dependent on his society
> for his soul-evolution?... It had always been like
> this, for him-a hunger after the things of the soul, in
> which other preoccupation's were submerged.... To
> him love was freedom of heart (p. 11).

The narrator informs us that

> A woman in the village of Motabeng paralleled his
> [Sello's] inner development. Most of what applied
> to Sello applied to her, because they were twin souls
> with closely-linked destinies and the same capacity
> to submerge other preoccupation's in a pursuit after
> the things of the soul (p. 11).

Sello and Dan were the two sides of Elizabeth. Her spiritual struggle with these evil powers made her suffer mental breakdown twice. Recurrent in her subconscious Sello and Dan become hallucinatory symbols turning her life into a nightmare. "Dan" she says "understood the mechanics of power. From his gestures, he clearly thought he had a wilting puppet in his hands." (p. 13) Sello is her guardian angel, he tells her "love isn't like that; Love is two people mutually feeding each other"(p. 14). This thought or idea is to occur again and again guiding Elizabeth throughout her soul-journey until she is able to make that ultimate "sharp, short leap to freedom."[11]

Elizabeth narrates how she became a pawn in the hands of Sello, Dan, and Medusa. She was born in South Africa. It was at a mission school where she was placed in her childhood that the inauspicious circumstances surrounding her birth were callously revealed to at her

> Your mother was insane. If you're not careful you'll
> get insane just like your mother. Your mother was a
> white woman. They had to lock her up, as she was
> having a child by the stable boy, who was a native."
> (p.16)

This was her first rude awakening to "the details of life and oppression in South Africa."

For a few years she quietly lived on the edge of South Africa's life. She spent some time living with Asian families, where she learnt about India and its philosophies, and some time with a German woman from "whom she learnt about Hitler and Jesus and the Second World War. A year before her marriage she tentatively joined a political party. It was banned two days later and in the state of emergency which was declared she was searched and briefly arrested.

Elizabeth married "a gangster just out of jail, who said he had thought deeply about life while in prison. But soon women were complaining of being molested by him. After a year, Elizabeth picked up her small boy and walked out of the home. Through a newspaper advertisement she got a teaching post in Botswana and she took "an exit permit, which like her marriage, held the never return clause." The above are the necessary data Elizabeth herself provides for the reader to understand her circumstances. The source of her nightmarish existence are the circumstances of her birth in an oppressive racist society, where being Black tantamounts to a congenital sickness, and a disastrous marriage that barely lasted a year. Both spell out her double yoke. Elizabeth learns to defend herself by resorting to madness. She suffered periodic mental breakdowns.

Elizabeth says that it was in Botswan "where, mentally, the normal and the abnormal blended completely" in her mind. "It was barely three months after her arrival in the village of Motabeng when her life began to pitch over from an even keel, and it remained from then onwards at a pitchedover angle." (p. 21). The bulk of the narrative is about Elizabeth's agony, her baptism by fire which prepared her for the knowledge of the truth. Her dream images include Egyptian Greek, Roman, and Oriental gods-Medusa, Osiris, Buddha, and "the brotherhood of man." In her clear moments she makes revealing statements about her experiences. For example, she welcomes her suffering in this thought:

> It seemed to her as though all suffering gave people and nations a powerful voice for the future and a common meeting-ground ... the Gods' turned out on observation to be ordinary, practical, sane people, seemingly their only distinction being that they had consciously concentrated on spiritual earnings (p. 31).

Sometimes she resented the agony. For example looking at her son she thought:

> Journeys into the soul are not for women with

children, not all that dark heaving turmoil. They are
for men, and the toughest of them took off into the
solitude of the forests and fought out their battles
with hell in deep seclusion. No wonder they hid
from view. *The inner life is ugly* (p. 50). (Italics are
mine).

Elizabeth survived to become a strong, powerful spiritual being, well
grounded in the things of the spirit. She, like Tutuola's Palm-wine drunkard, has
been to the land of the dead and is back armed not only with insight but with a
remedy for triumphant living. Lawrence's famous poem[12] provides the words to
express that triumphant feeling welling up in her soul:

Not I, but the wind that blows through me! A fine
wind is blowing the new direction of time. If only I
let it bear me ... if only, most lovely of all, I yield
myself and am borrowed by the wind that takes its
course through the chaos of the world ... Oh, for the
wonder that bubbles into my soul (p. 205).

Elizabeth tells us how she survives her ordeal:

It wasn't any kind of physical stamina that keep her
going, but a vague, instinctive pattern of normal
human decencies combined with the work she did,
the people she met each day and the unfolding of a
project with exciting inventive (p. 146).

Elizabeth's survival was aided by three other women encountered in *A
Question of Power*. Through their interaction with Elizabeth we learn a lot about
female bonding,[13] a central concept in feminist ideology. One woman alone
cannot survive the onslaught of exploitation and abuse often meted out to women,
but with the aid of other women, healing, and self affirmation are realized.

We encounter two Danish ladies in the novel. Camilla is evil whilst
Brigette, on the other hand, counteracts her as a benevolent force. Both act as foils
for Elizabeth. Camilla who is working as an Agricultural Officer in Botswana, is a
negative influence on Elizabeth. She reminds her of the hypocrisy and arrogance

of whites in South Africa. She recoils from her who she refers to as "the half-mad Camilla woman" and "Rattlè-tongue." In her portrayal Bessie Head presents the image of a frustrated and insensitive woman who needs to acquire humility. Through the openness of Elizabeth and Brigette, she is redeemed.

Brigette is the opposite of Camilla. Elizabeth finds in her a twin soul, a kindred spirit with whom she could relate. Their brief contact is a symbiotic experience of spiritual growth. Talking to Elizabeth Birgette says "Life is such a gentle, treasured thing. I learn about it every minute. I think about it so deeply." (p. 81) She agrees with Elizabeth's comments on suffering in South Africa that "the faces of the oppressed people are not ugly" even though the torturers become more hideous day by day. "Who is the greater man-the man who cries, broken by anguish, or his scoffing, mocking, jeering oppressor?" (p. 84) Elizabeth asks rhetorically. Birgette agreeing says to Elizabeth

> You say everything I have in my own heart.... But I cannot express myself so well because I have never suffered. I see suffering. It hurts me.

She is not renewing her contract because the suffering she sees around her affects her emotionally.

Birgette is a correction of the impression one gets from Camilla. It is not true that one only becomes sensitive to suffering for having suffered. What is necessary is an openness and sympathetic attitude towards life. Of course, the society nourishes this, hence the major difference Elizabeth identifies between herself and Birgette is not race but the fact that one belongs to a progressive society whilst the other belongs to a morally decadent one. She surmises:

> The human soul is alone in the battle of life. It is helped ... by profoundly moral social orders, such as Moses established for the Jews.... The questions of tenderness, love, appeal, compassion, truth, still lie within (p. 86).

While Birgette enables Elizabeth to work out answers to some fundamental questions that have bothered her Kenosi was an agent of life and regeneration. Her simple outlook on life is nourished by the humaneness of the society in which she was raised. That society exalts life above all things.

Kenosi came into Elizabeth's life at a time when she was approaching a mental breakdown and she was concerned about her son's well being in the event of her illness. Kenosi, who was about Elizabeth's age had no difficulty loving the little boy. "It was a way of village life.... Children were caressed and attended to, their conversations were listened to with affectionate absorption" (p. 88). Elizabeth was to look back at Kenosi's sudden appearance as "one of the miracles or accidents that saved her life" (p. 89). Observing her closely Elizabeth remarks:

> Her movements were extraordinarily quiet, soft, intensely controlled.... She was really an exceedingly beautiful woman in strength and depth of facial expression, in knowingness and grasp of life; its joys, its expected disillusionment. She was really the super-wife, the kind who would keep a neat, ordered house and adore in a quiet, undemonstrative way both the husband and children.

Perhaps Kenosi's statement about herself is a clue to her beautifully coordinated life-"I work with my hands," she said, proudly. "I have always worked. I do any kind of work." Kenosi and Elizabeth became business partners, working miracles in the production of all kinds of fresh vegetables, even growing "Cape Gooseberries" in Botswana and gradually introducing the peasant women there to profit oriented economy.

After one of Elizabeth's crises, when "her head exploded into a thousand fragments of fiery darkness'" and she lay in bed for two days barely conscious, Kenosi came around. She sat down on a chair beside the bed. "She was silent, self-contained alertly practical." She was concerned about the rain storm which caused water to over-run the beds of tomatoes. She later said to Elizabeth, "you must never leave the garden ... I cannot work without you." This quiet expression of affection and need for her jolted Elizabeth out of her mental stupor. She thought "the way this woman brought her back to life and reality!"

Elizabeth indirectly pays full tribute to Kenosi in attributing to her both her full recovery, mental sanity as well as a new vision of life. She says, at sunset when work with Kenosi at the garden was over and everything was peaceful it was then she began to jot down the fragmentary notes "such as a ship-wrecked sailor might make on a warm sandy beach as he stared back at the stormy sea that had nearly taken his life." It is at this point that she sings her "Magnificent" referred to earlier "Not I, but the wind that blows through me!" Her song glorifies bonding between women which enables them to survive.

Elizabeth's presentation in *A Question of Power* is Bessie Head's most sustained and complete dramatization of her philosophy of "sanctifying affliction" and her conviction about women's strength.

## THE COLLECTOR OF TREASURES

Bessie Head's final fictional work is a collection of short stories entitled *The Collector of Treasures*. The short story is a flexible form which allows the writer a quick and focused treatment of chosen themes. A number of memorable female characters emerge in *The Collector of Treasures* which is a collection of thirteen moving short stories. Together the stories become a drawing together of all the various images of women that we have encountered in Head's fictional world. There is Dikeledi whose pride, independence, and appetite for living act as a catalyst for others. There is Life whose rebellious spirit leads her to challenge the social order of the patriarchal and racist community in which she lives. We have women of all ages, traditional women who under the burden of custom, have learnt to survive and take care of their needs. But we also encounter the beer drinkers who find marriage boring and enslaving. Through this group the writer explores the negative tendency among modern women and the degenerating influence of prostitution

The men come off badly as the ones who help to destroy homes. In the most moving story which gives the collection its title, Dikeledi is the beautiful soul who collects treasures. She suffers but never looses hold of her dignity, her warmth, friendship, and eagerness to share draw people towards her. Her imprisonment is a symbol of physical and psychological imprisonment of women, their emasculation by the inimical systems. Head, however, portrays through Dikeledi that even in prison, in an anti-heroic situation, a woman can still achieve heroic proportion. This is very important because it is the first time we encounter an anti-heroic heroine in African Literature. Achebe and most of our writers, present Aristotelian heroes but Head's anti-hero is made heroic.

## CONCLUSION

The three identified preoccupation's that direct as well as empower Head's fictional world are the dehumanizing of Black people in South Africa, the experiences of women under oppression and the individual's struggle for self-liberation. All three impinge on one another, for Head has identified the cause of African men's inhuman treatment of their women to be due to the frustration of history.[14] Disadvantages of history, however, are not sufficient excuse for the continuity of decadence. Like Paul Thebolo, the men must seek within themselves "the power to create themselves anew." Each of the novels has dramatized a spiritual journey towards liberation. In some of them this spiritual journey involves a man, however, his agent of vision leading him towards self fulfillment is a woman. The highest compliment paid to womanhood in her works is the creation of Elizabeth. Through her sufferings she emerges as the visionary of a new world. The challenge to continue to affirm human goodness in spite of everything. Like Dikeledi our lives must be filled "with treasures of kindness and love" gathered in our inter-action with one another.

The message that comes through her fictions is that living is a spiritual journey towards liberation and greater enlightenment: that suffering sanctifies the oppressed whilst it disfigures the oppressor. But the great leap to personal freedom is not reserved for one race alone. It is what makes one really human. These are not new themes, in fact, they are the most popular themes of literature from its very beginning in Oral Traditions and the great European and oriental literary tradition through to the most significant and revolutionary literature of our time being produced in the Third World. What is significant about Bessie Head's work is that she focuses on women, whereas the protagonists of the great novels that come to mind-*Don Quiote*, *Robinson Crusoe*, and *A Hundred Years of Solitude*-are men. Head's treatment of her theme, the formal precision and assuredness with which her novels are executed make them compulsory reading.

We are impressed by her narrative strategies such as the use of symbols[15] the orality of the language of her ordinary people recreating the real life speech style in the African villages: the lively dialogue and the unintrusive voice of the omniscient narrator which directs our response rather than interfere with the narrative process. All these blend together making for the resonance of the main message which echoes throughout all her works. Her main message is that

> ... all suffering gave people and nations a powerful
> voice for the future and a common meeting-
> ground.[16]

In all her writing women's sufferings leave their imprint on our consciousness. At the same time they are portrayed as the ones "who have the strength to build a new world." Head allows us to experience the difficulties and struggles of her female characters, eventually to enable us to celebrate their victories as women who surmount their oppressed situations

Head's work proves conclusively the statement that:

> Individual awareness and consciousness of their
> subordinate position has always existed among
> individuals or groups of women. It is only when this

becomes evident through collective action by large
numbers of women that it can be said that a feminist
movement exists.[17]

Do I dare to suggest that women writers like Bessie Head have paved the
way for the emergence of strong feminist movements in our continent that will
transform our lives.

## FOOTNOTES

1.   *When Rain Clouds Gather.* 1968. Penguin Books Ltd.: U.K.
     *Maru,* 1971. Heinemann: London.
     *A Question of Power.* 1974. Heinemann: London.
     *The Collector of Treasures and Other Botswana Village Tales.*
     1977.Heinemann: London.
     *Serowe Village of the Rain Wind.* 1991. Heinemann: London.
     *A Bewitched Crossroads.* 1984. A. D. Donker Ltd.: Cape Town, South
     Africa.

2.   Eilersen, Gillian Stead ed. 1989. *Tales of Tenderness and Power.* A.D.
     Donker: Cape Town, South Africa.
     Mackenzie, Craig. ed. 1990. *A Woman Alone: Autobiographical Writings.*
     Heinemann: Oxford.
     Vigne, Randolph ed. 1991. *A Gesture of Belonging.* Heinemann: London.
     1993. *The Cardinals, with Meditations and Short Stories.* M. J. Daymond:
     Cape Town.
     Eilersen, Gillian Stead. 1995. *Bessie Head: Thunder Behind Her Ears.*
     David Philip Publishers Ltd.: South Africa.

3.   Donvan, J. 1989. *Feminist Literary Criticism.* University of Kentucky
     Press. p. 74.

4.   1977. *The Collector of Treasures.* All page references are to
     the Heinemann ed.

5.   Ibid.

6.   Ibid.

7.   Rhoda Reddock. 1988. "Feminism and Feminist Thought: An Historical
     Overview" in *Gender in Caribbean Development.* P. Mohamed and C.
     Shepherd (ed.). UWI.

8    Nichols, Lee (ed.). 1981. *Conversations with African Writers.* Voice of

America: Washington D.C.

9.      1971. All page references are to *Maru* Heinemann: London.

10.     Nichols, Lee (ed.) *Op.cit*.

11.     1974. All page references are to *A Question of Power*. Heinemann:
        London.

12      Lawerence, D. H. 1960. "Not I, Not I, But the Wind That blows Through
        Me!" in *The Faber Book of Modern Verse* ed. Michael Roberts: London.

13      Bonding among women is a familiar theme in the writings of African
        Americans. It is found in Alice Waler's *The Color Purple*, Toni Morrison's
        *Beloved*, and Paule Marshall's *Praise Song For the Widow*. It occurs in
        Ama Ata Aidoo's *Changes* as well. Bonding is related to the theme of
        healing which is the essential difference between Western feminist
        literature and the womanist alternative adopted by Black writers.

14.     *The Collector of Treasures*. pp. 91-93.

15.     In *Maru* as in *To The Light House* by Virginia Woolf, Margaret Cadmore's
        painting is the most eloquent representation of her thought and helps to
        clarify the message of that novel. In *A Question of Power*, the womb, the
        images of Buddha, Medusa are some of the significant symbols.

16.     *A Question of Power*. p. 31.

17.     Rhoda Reddock, *Op. cit*.

# CHAPTER THREE

## Zulu Sofola: A Champion of Tradition in a Dislocated World
### Adeola James

When Zulu Sofola died a year ago, shortly after the demise of her husband, death took away one of Africa's most dynamic fighters for women's rights and for their recognition. Her fight was not mere rhetoric, she backed it up with admirable creativity as a playwright and director of both drama and choral performances. Her struggle for the empowerment of women is evidenced in copious dramatic output and critical statements. It is some comfort that these works will long survive her and will carry on the message of her life. This essay, then, is a tribute to a dear friend for whom I have the greatest admiration. It is a general exploration of Sofola's plays, highlighting her basic concerns and her contribution to African Literature.

A reading of Sofola's titles locates here interests in a variety of ills that afflict the Nigerian society. She examines and dramatizes conflict of cultures the tragedy of a civil war, the anachronistic position of women, corruption, academic pretensions, and other manifestations of moral failure. She engages herself with the here and now in such a deeply personal way that her agonizing concern about the destiny of her nation is communicated with distinct immediacy. In an interview she remarks that her temperament does not suit the detailed probing into moods, "when I start I want to go and I went what I have to say to come right out."[1] This quick motion and a certain aura of urgency characterize her work. In these plays, as if with the quick banging of the hammer, she moves her observing, critical eye around society, forcing her compatriots to see their folly sometimes through comic, satirical lenses, sometimes through tragic ones. At all times the plays are entertaining and forceful.

Sofola wrote about a dozen plays. These dramatic output falls into three categories. Some of these plays can be discussed as comedies, others as tragedies and two are open-ended in their deliberate ambiguity. Whatever form she adopts, her faith in our traditions is often unmistakable. In her visions it appears we have opened ourselves to the malaise of modern society by neglecting our ancient traditions. The process of making this unifying statement is explored in this essay.

## *THE DISTURBED PEACE OF CHRISTMAS*

*The Disturbed Peace of Christmas* was published in 1971. It is a simple comedy woven around the Christian message of the birth of Christ, "the Prince of Peace." Ironically, this message of peace is disturbed by the conception of another child, this time, not an immaculate conception but as a result of a clandestine affair between the two main characters, Mary and Joseph, who are rehearsing the Nativity play. It is to be staged in the community to convey to the people the message of peace.

The performance of the play is threatened when the angry parents withdraw both Mary and Joseph blaming the late rehearsals as the setting for Mary's pregnancy. Good sense prevails in the end and the play is performed with great success. A crisis is averted as everyone, even Titi and Ayo as Mary and Joseph respectively, in reenacting the Christmas message, each sees his/her personal problem in a new light.

*The Disturbed Peace of Christmas* is a morality play. The plot is clever and adds to the interest of an otherwise uncomplicated play. Part of its entertainment lies in its faithful recreation of a play rehearsal in process. The typical confusion which prevails and which miraculously disappears at the premier performance lends credibility to the dramatist's art. The appropriate use of language and the humor adds to the play's interest. The echo of everyday language suffuses the play adding to its authenticity. For example, here Ladipo is rebuking his son for his lack of discretion:

| | |
|---|---|
| Ladipo: | Boy, speak up because you have put yourself into trouble. |
| Ayo: | I did not know that would happen. |
| Ladipo: | You did not know what would happen? |
| Ayo: | We did not expect anything to happen. |
| Ladipo: | A man fools around with a girl and he does not know that something would happen? (pp. 18-19) |

Ladipo's advice to his son Ayo is indirectly for the audience. He says to him "... develop a mind of your own. Believe in what is good, search for it, and finding it, hold fast to it. Nothing is as disturbing to inner peace as a truth lost because of lack of strength of mind."

## THE WIZARD OF LAW

The concern for her society is the motivating impulse behind Sofola's dramatic creations. This concern is implicit even in what appears to be only a light comedy. *The Wizard of Law* published in 1957, appears to be pure entertainment. It is a farce poking fun at two significant ailments in the Nigerian society namely: dishonesty which is blatantly manifested by the legal practitioners everywhere and an absurd form of materialism which cuts across the whole society.

Sikira no longer respects her husband because after their marriage she discovers that he is not as prosperous as she had thought. She complains about having to "dress like a beggar to the praying ground." She made the confession that:

> It thought he had something so I agree to be his
> wife. I married him and refused the hand of
> Mamuck and Adamin because I thought he was
> shaking money in his pockets when he was shaking
> keys ... I could have been the wife of a big man
> today. I could have been riding in big shiny cars
> today.

What are the basis of a marital union? What are the criteria upon which one chooses a marriage partner? The audience asks. Sikira's self-revelation is frightening because of its frankness. These statements are not made in jest, they are the avowed criteria. Although sociologists still idealize the African marriage institution as one binding families together; however, the mystery of that institution, so hallowed by our forefathers, is being flouted and abused today. Unions like that between Sikira and Ramomi seem to be the norm. As one who holds sacred the institutions and practices of our forefathers, might the dramatist not be hinting that the root of the confusion and mindlessness experienced in our societies today is inherent in the disrespect for the sacred values that sustained previous generations?

The legal professions comes in for its own criticism in the satirized figure of Ramoni—"that wizard of the Court of Law." Ramoni believes that his benevolent fortune has changed because of the witchcraft practiced on him by Momodu who "with his evil power ... confused my head." (p. 2) "The wizard of Law" therefore turns into a schemer because in a materialistic society where one's attire determines the kind of respect accorded to one, he says "wives of men like me should be wearing lace, damask and sanyan olomi golu, not pomki." In order to buy expensive materials befitting his wife's status as a lawyer's wife, he has to resort to scheming and stealing. His cleverness as a lawyer is not based on the power of his legal argument but on his ability to feign and defraud. The degradation of the world society is exposed through the dramatized statement that corruption cuts right through all levels of the society. Rafiu rejoices and thanks

"Allah, God" because he manages to get '20 a meter for cloth that would have cost 10 a metre." He revels in his windfall saying "Dese big men know book for nothing. God don throw me plenty money today ... I don chop plenty money today-o." With this in mind, one does not feel sorry for Rafiu, when it turns out that he meets his match in Ramoni "the Wizard of Law" who, after securing some metres of lace materials for nothing, also uses his twisted legal argument to free Akpan from blame for stealing Rafiu's two goats. The audience's enjoyment of this cycle of dishonesty and theft is at its height when at the end even Akpan, who has been so cleverly defended by Ramoni, refuses to pay the legal fee. Using Ramoni's own argument to defraud, "he has been turned into a goat during the nine months that Rafiu forced him to live with goats and only knows to bleat like a goat." When "the Wizard of Law" fails to extort his fees from a bleating goat one feels that justice is done in an unjust world.

*The Wizard of Law* is a perfect farce, its clever handling and careful orchestration make it a roaring success. However, its primary function which is to question the values and morals of professionals and individual members of the society should not be lost sight of amidst the candid humour. A number of elements contribute to the success of the play both as a theatrical piece and as a moral story. One is the use of familiar tricks from the traditional folktales. There are reminiscences of the tortoise and Anansi when Ramoni feigns illness. The techniques employed by Ben Jonson, which makes *Volpone* so remarkable, come to mind as one looks at *The Wizard of Law*. Apart from the characters taking the audience into their confidence in their tricks, one cannot think of Ramoni as anything else but a fox. The fox, the tortoise, Brer Nansi-are these not the characters that dominate our societies today, even our politics? The play invites the viewer, in a very concrete way, to ask where he/she fits in whether as Sikira, Ramoni, Rafiu, or even Akpan. There is no room for mindless enjoyment, the dramatist seems to imply that there is a lot of room for change.

## THE SWEET TRAP

*The Sweet Trap*, published in 1977, is the next comedy. In this play the dramatist focuses on "the women question." The discussion about Okebadan[2] and the disgust expressed by Clara and Mrs. Ajala opens the play, paving the way for the theme which is the struggle for equality between the sexes and an end to the traditional male supremacy. The conflict of interest is encapsulated in the different attitudes adopted towards Oke-Ibadan festival. The female protagonists felt that the festival provides men an opportunity to ridicule women thus reaffirming male supremacy. As such it is a "primitive festival" that must be abolished. In men's view, however, Okebadan proves "that our forefathers understood the value of psychological and emotional release of tensions. [It] is the epitome of their understanding of the human psyche." Clara and Fatima have adopted the new militant posture towards the man/woman relationship. This is revealed in their marriage. Clara, addressing her husband over his objection to her holding a birthday party, responds: "Did you think I would blindly accept orders from you without scrutinizing them first?" Later she adds:

> you should have known that with my degree, I
> cannot be pushed around by the inflated ego of an
> undisciplined male partner. I stand on equal grounds
> with you and cannot be forced into any action that is
> against good reasoning (p. 10).

In similar assertive frame of mind Fatima boasts that her husband has just learnt "a new truth" ... "that I will buy what I want and do what I want whether or not he has given approval" (p.24).

Mrs. Jinadu differs from both Clara and Fatima. Although she is a university graduate, she says her happiness is in what she can do to make her husband happy. "If he says no and I see that he will be unhappy if I go against his will, I immediately abandon my plans" (p. 24). The climax of the play is the abortive birthday celebration which breaks the ranks of the rebellious women who turn against one another. The resolution of the play sees the men triumphant, thus reestablishing the male ego and the maintaining of the status quo. Fatima acknowledges the royal position of the male saying "my mother had always taught me that a woman's husband is her crown and it is her duty to protect that crown." Symbolically, Clara accepts that authority when she kneels down and apologizes to her husband as the play ends.

What is the central statement of the play? Its realistic texture and the dialogue, borrowed from familiar daily altercations everywhere in the Nigerian society, make the play very entertaining. At a higher level of sensibility one is led to suspect a satirical intention directed, on the one hand, at our men, and on the other, at the women too. The play ridicules all the "Dr. Jinadu," and "Dr. Ogegunle" and "Dr. Sotubo" and "Professor Eriko" of our society. In spite of their learning, their enlightenment is only skin-deep because their attitude to the womenfolk remains backward. One is led to this conclusion from Dr. Sotubo's statement to his wife:

> Get it into your head once and for all that your university education does not raise you above the illiterate fish seller in the market. Your degree does not make the slightest difference. You are a woman and must be treated as a subordinate. Your wishes, your desire and your choices are subject to my pleasure and mood. Anything I say is law and unalterable (p. 10).

There is a lot of satirical connotation implied in this statement. There is no doubt that there are many men who think this way even at this threshold of the twenty-first century. Implicit in the play is the suggestion that this sort of backward attitude is detrimental to progress. The writer's satirical weapon is not inflicted on men alone, women are made to see how their pettiness undermines their struggle for fair treatment. Clara, with her university degree, is not only condescending towards, but also spiteful of Fatima who has only primary school education. Superficial class snobbery weakens the solidarity of the women.

Sofola's message here is at one with the finding of her counterpart in Tanzania-the Swahili dramatist-Penina Mhadndo.[3] Both suggest that women need to transcend jealousy and social differences in order to successfully tackle the question of gender inequality. It is commendable when women can dissect their own ills dispassionately without romanticism.

## REVERIES IN THE MOONLIGHT

*Reveries in the Moonlight* adopts the form of the traditional moonlight games. It is saturated with the air of freedom and lightheartedness that characterize those games. In the traditional society, moonlight night is a period for romance when young girls dance in a ring, sing, and tell folktales and riddles under the watching eyes of the man in the moon. The play begins with some of the songs performed on such nights of fun. Although the spirit of jollification pervades the play, like the earlier ones discussed, it contains a serious social theme. Abiona has to choose for her husband either Otakoo, the eighty-year old man to whom she was betrothed from birth, or Ugo a young suitor. "He was the first to bight the first firewood immediately after I was born" she explains to her young suitor Ugo who rightly points out to her "That is wrong. If I had not been a baby then I would have been the first to bring your first firewood." Abiona remonstrates: "Yes, but Otakpo did it first. And he is my father's best friend. So I must marry him because of my father."

The dramatic action is played out in a light-hearted fashion and there is not doubt that this is one instance when the members of the audience are not expected to suspend their disbelief but simply to soak themselves in the ceremonial ritual that our foreparents have fashioned in celebration of the deity of the moon. There is a lot of dancing and singing and gossip about the romances in the village. Sofola captures this atmosphere beautifully and no one is sorry at the end that Otakpo loses out. It would have been outrageous were he to have won.

*Reveries in the Moonlight* is strongly reminiscent of Soyinka's *The Lion and the Jewel*. However, in Sofola's play this theme of conflict of choice between a traditional and a modern suitor is not developed with the same type of intensity as in the Soyinka play or even as in T*he Wedlock of the Gods*, another play in which Sofola treats a similar theme. This is not cited as a weakness, we are simply noting a differentiation of purpose and function among plays that might appear to be alike. One feels that the author's purpose in *Reveries in the Moonlight* is simply to capture the spirit of traditional moonlight entertainment.

The language of the drama is rich in imagery. For example, Otakpo justifying his claim on Abiona reasons thus:

> A man at my age deserves soft touches before bidding this painful world good-bye. The stones of life have battered me long enough. At a ripe old age of eighty the soft touches of a sweet maiden should soothe life's scars as sea breeze soothes the scourge of the mid-day sun.

We also encounter examples of people's beliefs when Onogwu tells Ndudi

> ... People have their different lives and destiny. If Abiona was the woman Ugo told his God he would marry, I can do nothing whatsoever about it.

*Reveries in the Moonlight* completes the list of the plays that can be described as comedies. When we turn to the tragedies, the contrast in the seriousness and handling of more perplexing situations are obvious. Sofola's versatility as a dramatist is fully demonstrated in the next category of plays which are technically more demanding.

## TRAGEDIES

### *WEDLOCK OF THE GODS*

*Wedlock of the Gods*, published in 1972, is one of Sofola's earliest tragedies. The drama is built around the theme of blighted love. This is a theme which is both ancient as well as universal. Within its temporal and spatial contexts, we are forced to ask some important questions regarding the validity of certain traditional practices in the contemporary world. We ponder on the position of women in the African society, as we agonize over the fate of both Ogwoma and Uloko.

Ogwoma and Uloko are two young lovers who break the traditional taboo surrounding mourning and have to pay the penalty with their lives. The dramatic conflict is situated in Ogwoma who is torn between filial duty and adherence to traditional marriage pattern on the one hand, and personal inclination on the other. Adigwu is her parent's choice because he can pay enough money needed for making the prescribed sacrifice for her sick brother's recovery. In spite of her protest Ogwoma "was tied and carried to Adigwu or whipped along the way like a ram to the alta" (p. 26). Thus a loveless marriage is solemnized. The reader's sympathy must be fully on Ogwoma's side and we desist from blaming her when the untimely death of Adigwu provides her with an opportunity to revert to Uloko, her own choice.

The conflict, though convincingly crafted is not compelling. There appears to be something forced about it, the weakness may well be in the dialogue that sometimes sounds banal. For example, in the following exchange notice how Ogwoma breaks the happy news of her pregnancy to Uloko that she is expecting his baby:

Ogwoma:      Look, Uloko, it is not time to tell you.

Uloko:         You must tell me ... Ogwoma,

|          | please, don't make my heart bleed. I have waited too long for you. Please, let me know what the future holds for me ... |
|----------|----------|
| Ogwoma:  | I did not want to tell you until after I have finished my plans. |
| Uloko:   | Please .... |
| Ogwoma:  | You would have seen it soon enough. |
| Uloko:   | Seen what, my love? |
| Ogwoma:  | It never hides .... |
| Uloko:   | My son is in there? |
| Ogwoma:  | Not so loud. |
| Uloko:   | Great God! ... My precious stone! My glorious one! (p. 12) |

The choice of words fails to typify the objective correlative of an atmosphere which is more conspicuously pregnant with tensions than with a child. In addition, the echo of Romeo and Juliet makes the reader somewhat skeptical. At the end when Uloko slays Odibei, drinks the rest of the poison given to Ogwoma and joins his lover in "a wedlock of the Gods," his parting elegy.

|          |          |
|----------|----------|
| Uloko:   | Ours is the wedlock of the gods. Together we shall forever be Lightning and thunder-inseparable! (p. 55-60) |

only rings true in the context of a folktale. It lacks the immediacy of a compelling dramatization of tragic waste of youth and promise.

The most authentic moment in the play is found in the tension created by

the abominable act of Ogwoma and Uloko. These tensions are convincingly
evoked and realized in the reaction of the elders who share common faith in the
traditions that bid them together. All the elders, including Ogwomna's own
mother, her mother-in-law and even Uloko's mother, agree that she has done the
abominable: "You are a man's wife, dead or alive." Ogwoman's failure to marry
Adigwu's brother is the worst taboo in the land, the punishment for which is "a
swelling of the body with water leaking from everywhere." Nobody will agree to
treat her and even after death no forest will accept her body. A meeting
summoned by Ogwoma's father to seek advice on how to deal with the problem
ends in recriminations and confusion. Amidst great ill-feelings Odibei put a curse
on Ogwoma. This later scenario is the part that grips. We are made to observe that
the greater burden of blame, pain, and suffering are borne by the women in their
various roles whether as the victim of ill-fated love (Ogwoma), or as the mother
of the unfortunate girl (Nneka), or as the unloved Adgwu's mother (Odibei) who
sees it as her responsibility to avenge the honour of her dead son. What about
Uloko's mother Ogoli, who sees her son trapped but is powerless to influence him.
Naturally and agonizingly, she vents her anger on Ogwoma fully exculpating her
son's guilt:

Ogoli:     Uloko knows what every well-
           trained son ought to know. She was
           given to a man as a wife. That was
           not enough to put an end to her hunt
           for my son. She will not let her
           marriage stop her. Her husband died,
           but rather than wait and let his spirit
           return to the world of the gods, she
           has enticed and dragged my son into
           an act of death.

Ogwoma:    I did not entice your son.

Ogoli:     A man goes to a woman; it is the

woman who opens the door (p. 23).

Dapo Adelugba[4] notes the occasional banality, but commends the "authentic imagery, diction and rhythm." However, being a male critic, Adelugba bails to see the essential core of the play as speaking to the sufferings of women, past and present, in the African societies, hence his conclusion that "... the play is altogether too simple and transparent for it to merit serious consideration in the genre of tragedy" (p. 209). The Wedlock of the Gods gains plausibility as a compelling tragedy only when viewed as a dramatization of the adversities faced by women in a society that is paradoxically resistant to change, especially, in the fundamentals of existence. The dramatist was once asked on whose side she was in the conflict, whether on the side of the young people who break the tradition or is she in favour of the rigid traditions. Her response was that if the young *must* break the old taboo, they *must* also be prepared to face the consequences.[5] This response underlines the tragic conflict that defies an easy resolution.

## OLD WINES ARE TASTY

*Old Wines are Tasty* (1974) dramatizes the tragic end of another young man who disrespects traditions. Okebuno is presented as a naive, western-educated and would be saviour of his people. His naivete and his basic ignorance of his people's traditions lead to his untimely elimination.

## THE LION AND THE JEWEL

Reminiscent of Lakunle in *The Lion and the Jewel*, Okebuno, in this instance, lost not only in the political game to his rival Okolo, but also lost his life. The play is set in a Nigerian village during the first Republic and it is contemporaneous in time and similar in mood with *The Lion and the Jewel*. Okebuno travels to his village from Lagos to canvass for support for the forthcoming elections. Instead of a warm welcome, he discovers a strong opposition and manipulation that eventually drives him to his death.

The dramatic conflict arises from the contrast in thought, feeling and outlook between Okebuno, on the one hand, the elders and their young, ambitious political manipulators, on the other. The great gulf between these two groups is exposed in an uncompromisingly strong language. In Okebuno's view, the elders are "senile men" who are blinded to truth by "thin webs of anachronistic tradition:"

> Okebuno:   Men out there in the world don't look
> into the future backwards. They do
> not allow thin webs of anachronistic
> tradition to blind them to truth. This
> country is on the upsurge for
> modernity, progress and civilization,
> not interested in how to greet senile
> men (p. 21).

Okebuno is so over-confident in his western qualifications that he dismisses the local traditions as "primitive initiation:"

> Okebuno:   ... because I have not greased your
> palms with bush rats and chicken
> feet your primitive initiation has
> suddenly become very important.
> People that matter, those who know
> where the world is going, chose me
> to represent you because they know
> my basic qualification (p. 37).

Okebuno disparagingly says of the elders that they wear "hoods of witchcraft," growing wings at night whilst "... people out there in the world wear academic gowns; they wear crowns of knowledge; they wear hoods of degrees ... (p. 44).

To the elders, Okebuno is an upstart, an ignorant "small boy" who should be ignored:

Ogbelani:        ... this boy should have been told
some things before now.
Lagos is a no man's land. Small boys
become beings there
but not here in Olona. We have
tradition, we have a system (p. 35).

Sarcastically, the elder adds "these boys have been in town for the past two days but we don't know them, we have not seen them," Okebuno's ignorance of the traditional speech pattern is again revealed when he interprets this statement literally and holds up the elder as a liar. This ignorance is indicative of his alienation. Akwagwu advises his nephew that "It is old wines that are tasty, not the new. You have tasted in whiteman's country-wines brewed only yesterday, but know our wine so that you may know what to mix with it" (p. 44).

Okebuno's failure to heed this advice leads to his tragic destruction. His tragic flaws are his ignorance of his tradition, his hasty dismissal of its value; his disrespect for the elders and his immaturity. Confronted with the wily machinations of his political opponents he becomes completely confused, loses his bearing and ultimately his life.

Ukebnuno is presented as a tragic figure. His tragedy, however, claims other victims. His mother Anyasi and his young wife Ndudi are also victims. In their circumstances they rightly feel abandoned by the death of the only person in whom their hope of social well being is reposited. The villagers, too, are victims of their own rigid and inflexible mode of life. They will continue to live in darkness in a world that has been illumined by new ideas, inventions, and changes. This illumination remains unavailable to them because of their stubborn grip on outmoded, unproductive world view. Tragically they are turning their backs on life-enhancing possibilities.

There is yet another tragic note in the play, that is what appears to be an unbridgeable gap between traditional Africa and the modern dispensation which our western-educated youths have acquired. There is a disturbing contradiction in that the elders encourage their children to acquire this education which eventually alienate them. Sofola dramatizes this contradiction pungently, but offers no solution. The contradiction is even more pervasive today with the collapse of our economy and the lure of North America and Europe as the nirvana for everyone.

There is a subtle reference to sexism in the African society where the mother is blamed for all the offenses committed by the children. Ogbelani rebukes Okebuno's uncle saying.

> Akuagwu should have let his father's people handle him. He is only his mother's brother and as long as Olona is still Olona, women will still be women. I am sure that had his father's people trained him he would have known and done what every man is supposed to do (p. 32).

Yet the only voice of reason, in all the uncontrolled passion is that of Okebuno's mother who pleads:

> Anyasi:      Son, a leader handles his people as
>              one handles fire, the heat must be
>              controlled or it may devour. Handle
>              this problem with good sense (p. 44).

Had this advice been heeded instead of treating his mother with the usual disregard that women are accustomed to expect from men, the tragedy might have been averted.

The theme of culture conflict has been immortalized in the works of Achebe, Soyinka, and Okot p'Bitek. *In Old Wines are Tasty* Sofola presents a women's version of that theme. She locates the source of the present confusion in arrested economic and social development, political, moral, and spiritual bankruptcy that are caused by the colonial intervention. Since drama does not allow for authorial voice, the author adopts a multiple point of view. All the characters are victims of either their own ignorance or the ignorance and meanness of others. We notice that the two political opponents are not polarized, ideologically. Here Sofola captures the reality of the Nigerian political life in which ideology has never been a serious dividing line. Nigeria has always been the victim of self-appointed leaders whose real motive for seeking power is to gain access to the national money bag. The picture painted in the play is bleak and it reminds one of the agonizing statement uttered by the dramatist[6] at a conference some years ago. Referring to her country she said "no human beings live there." Far from being a preposterous statement, it is an expression of the collective frustration and rage. If the play offers us no solution, it cannot be dismissed as invaluable. One hopes that out of the statement and restatement of all Africa's present contradictions and confrontations will come a valid answer one day. The momentum that is gathering leads many to believe that we are approaching that African solution, not only at the national level but continent-wide.

## KING EMENE AND QUEEN OMU

If *Wedlock of the Gods* and *Old Wines are Tasty* are tragedies created from social and political conditions, *King Emene* and *Queen Omu* are historical tragedies dealing, as the author indicates, with specific incidents in the Nigerian national history. *King Emene* dramatizes the tragedy that ensues from the King's violation of some traditional practices connected with the celebration of the Week of Peace. Ezedibie explains the significance of the Peace Week:

> Our forefathers taught us that the Peace Week is a week when man and the goads become one. Our King is that man who becomes one with the gods for us so that he can tell our gods our problems and see to it that the good things of life come to us. He is to drive away evil spirits for us (p. 42).

King Emene, like Okebuno and Ogwoma, Sofola's characters who have defied tradition, appeals to the audience for sympathy proffering valid reasons for his defiance. He is distrustful of the elders who are the custodians of the traditional practices. He explains that:

> Only two months after my coronation they have
> resumed where they stopped with my father .... The
> have advised me against entering the Peace Week
> and ushering in the new year and the Omu has
> foolishly allowed herself to be used as their
> mouthpiece .... My father, for whatever reason he
> had to follow their advice, met with an untimely
> death at their hands. I am not going to make the
> same blunder (pp. 11-12).

In spite of this lucid analysis King Emene, who is presented as strong in his convictions, still meets with a calamity that engulfs the whole community. The impression one is left with is the unyielding strength of these ancient traditional beliefs and the strangulating hold they have on the people.

The King is deemed to have rebelled against the traditions of his forefathers in exiling the Omu and arbitrarily selecting another person, unconfirmed by the goddess, to consult the Oracle. Ojei, one of the elders, points out that:

> ... No King, with no matter what strength and
> influence, has the power to tell the Oracle who must
> receive messages from her. Omu has always
> consulted the oracles during the Peace week as far
> as one can remember (p.11).

Even thought the King's maneuver is in the interest of his own survival, one man's survival is of little importance when pitted against a possible communal disaster. In the organizational logic of the play, it is revealed that the King's mother has committed a murder which has cast a spell of failure on the son's reign. Even in the absence of this causal element the hold that tradition has on the people would have created insurmountable problems for anyone who wishes to deviate. Hence, rather than seeing King Emene as a tragedy of a rebellion, it is more appropriate to see it as a tragedy of an intransigent and corrupt advocacy of ancient traditions. The elders are not cast in an admirable

light, their love of intrigues and selfish motives certainly make them abhorrent. They appear to exploit tradition for their own selfish ends and this makes them repugnant. Ironically these elders themselves do disservice to our ancient traditions. As is the case in *Old Wines are Tasty*, the dramatic statement is that even tradition becomes suspect and undependable when people manipulate it for selfish ends.

The language of the play is true to the tradition which it imitates-deep, gnomic language of the elders and poetic salutations suffuse the rich dialogue. Here is Ojei greeting the King:

> Greetings to you, my son, who is born into wealth,
> One to whom money is plenty like sand,
> One who when he stands on the road nobody passes.
> The lion of his kingdom,
> The fear of his peers,
> The King of Oligbo, ...
>
> The son of the line of leopards,
> The indomitable son of him whom kings fear to challenge.
> King Emene.
> I salute you (p. 30)!

Another interesting feature of *King Emene* is the prominent position occupied by women in the tragedy. The King's defiance of the Omu and the oracular goddess triggers off the conflict that finally destroys him.

If in *King Emene* we have a foretaste of the power of women in that society, *Queen Omu-Ako of Issele-Oligbo* is a celebration of that power in all its richness and complexity. The play dramatizes the courageous, though abortive, defense of the young sons of Asaba by the women folks during the Biafra war. The women's dynamism and courage is portrayed at all levels. For example, we have the goddess protecting and directing the movements of her children. Iyese-Omu involves her at the beginning of the action:

> Goddess Mkpitime,

Mother of all mothers,
Mother at war time,
Mother at peace time,
Mother who never deserts her children
We are facing enemies of War!
Let us not see death!

One of the most arresting images in the play is that of the young mother who has just given birth, covered with blood. The nurse commands in defiance: "Don't touch a mother who is still bleeding from child birth! Don't touch her."

The young mother, too, defying all fear, demands to be left alone:

Leave me alone! Don't kill me!
Don't kill my child! We have not done
anything to you! Don't kill us!

Her blood-covered body, fresh from childbirth, draws an unmistakable attention to the senseless slaughter in a fraternal war. Everywhere, women appear in solidarity and defiance. Another woman shouts "don't kill my husband as you killed by brothers." The women recognize their ultimate responsibility to preserve life hence their defiance of suffering:

Whatever one suffers
Let her endure it for her child.
Shedding of leaves does not kill the tree,
The python does not crush the ground to death,
Suffering for one's own child does not kill one.

At the head of them all, leading and guiding them is the Eze-Omu who brings out the essential difference between men and women:

Eze-Omu does not hide in the comfort of her palace
and watch her children destroyed by a frightened
king. The fire that will destroy my children should
also destroy me! Our Kings are frightened because
they are not mothers (p. 17).

Their goddess, of course, protects them from injuries:

It is a strange time when

> People talk in undertones
> people salute death with an embrace
> Brothers plant snakes
> Under the mats of brother!
> They talk in undertones,
> They smile with poison under their tongues,
> But the lioness of the sea understands them all.

The women's total faith in their goddess baffles and disarms the invading soldiers as revealed in the following dialogue:

| Benga: | Could there be some truth to the stories they carried about the goddess? |
|---|---|
| Otite: | Captain Raleigh confirmed the fact that a figure of a woman appears in the middle of the river dressed in white with outstretched arms. They say that every bullet sent in the direction of Agbor township is intercepted and disappears through the palms of her hands. Those that escape sink directly into the water. |
| Benga: | Do you really believe this? |
| Otite: | I don't, but the people do. That they all have escaped into their hiding places unhurt is noteworthy. |

The soldiers conclude:

| Benga: | These are strange people! |
|---|---|
| Otite: | As strange as their goddess. |

They even begin to fear the women:

"These women are spirits. They are dangerous." To my mind, *Queen Omu-Ako of Isele-Oligbo* stands at the pinnacle of Sofola's achievement. It is a celebration of traditional ritual which recalls, at its best, Soyinka's awesome achievement in *Death and the King Horseman*. It is a ritual performance that presents the viewer with the richness of oral tradition as we watch the dignified, awe-inspiring processions of women performing their rituals. They may be supplicating their goddess for protection or offering the symbolic white chalk to the invading Federal soldiers. The women's role is fundamental, they are the first on the stage and the last. The men take a second place, most of whom have run into hiding. It is a demonstration of the heroic power of our women which gives one a heightened appreciation of the daily heroism's of women. As mothers, workers or professionals they are the most sensitive members who keep the wheels of society rolling. The realistic evocation of the river goddess is triumphant, her invincibility is so strongly fixed in our consciousness that the bullet-ridden body of the Omu does not shake this faith; for Omu is only asleep, translated to that higher world where she will continue to protect her children.

In all these images Sofola demonstrates her strong commitment to the preservation of the tradition of her people as portrayed by these women, and her faith in women's strength. The unshakable faith reinforces her stature as a social critic. *Queen Omu-Ako of Issele-Oligbo* unifies and maximizes the various artistic manifestations in Sofola's earlier plays-her ability to draw on a wide variety of linguistic formulae, appropriate to whichever situation she wishes to depict; convincing portrayal of characters and a subtle deflation of self-importance. These qualities, noticeable in *Queen Omu*, render it not only one of Sofola's most satisfying works, but one that locates her interest primarily in the on-going struggle to appraise women's reality, their worth and achievement as truthfully as possible. Who is better placed than the female writer to do this? Sofola joins the rank of eminent writers like Ama Aidoo, Buchi Emecheta, and the late Bessie Head, to name the most successful, in locating and identifying, through their writings, the real strength of African womanhood.

## OPEN-ENDED PLAYS

### *SONG OF A MAIDEN*

*Song of a Maiden* is open-ended in its classification. Its enjoyment is derived from the contrast between the rich oral poetry in the chant of the priestess, the Bride's praise song and the lively dialogue in modern sophisticated, unpronounceable language of the academics.

The play polarizes the phony values of the academics against the genuine and natural existence of village life. The academics have chosen a village for performing their scientific experiments in astronomy. The villagers naturally were suspicious of the academics who have adopted the European ways and thrown away every quality that makes an "Omoluwabi." The villagers deliberate and here are some of their remarks:

> We all have known these book people long enough. They can read and read and write, but that is all. They have no head, they have no tail. There is nothing left in them that makes an Omoluwabi ....

> They called themselves our rulers and with the staff of power they have taken one by one everything that we called our own .... Who does not know that our children are now wilde animals? These people built schools, packed our children into them and turned our flesh and blood upside-down. Our children don't know us any more.

"They scorn everything we do even though they are natives of this country.... Our people were smelting iron before the knowledge they now boast of came to us.... Ogun, the great warrior mastered the art of warfare before these small boys knew their names."

The villagers, strengthened by their farsightedness, are willing to accommodate the academics. However, their goddess instructs that a ritual union between one of their village girls and one of the academics will make the latter acceptable in the village. Eccentric Professor Oduyinka is chosen for the ritual wedding. He, on his part, is unwilling to go through this "primitive" exercise which he regards as "infradignitatern and perfidy." His refusal throws confusion in the camp of the academics. In the debate that follows various academic issues are aired such as the worth of academic pursuits, Black dignity, capitalism versus socialism, traditionalism versus modernism, and the meaning of development.

Yetunde, whose family is selected by the goddess to produce a maiden for the wedding, bemoans her unfortunate lot since most of the young women in the village see Professor Oduyinka not only as a stranger but also as a mad man. Her parents protest the decision to give their daughter to "the book people" who cannot be trusted because they are "full of tricks and they kill without remorse."

The chief and other elders seem to have persuaded Alabi, Yetunde's father, to agree to the union, whilst Professor Oduyinka too has been coerced into agreement because the final scene of the play is a wedding scene. However, the wedding does not take place after all. The first contact between the couple elicits mutual feeling of revulsion, the note on which the play ends. This ending is a very effective dramatic tactic, carefully executed with facial expressions. It eloquently clinches the irreconcilability of both worlds-the false world of academic pretentiousness in contrast with the down-to-earth, humble and vibrant traditional acceptance of man's place in the universe. In this world view, man is only part of nature; not an arrogant master of it. His duty therefore is to continue to appease the goads and with prayers, sacrifices, and periodic observances negotiate for a peaceful co-existence with all other elements of the universe.

This play then appears to focus on the moral and intellectual bankruptcy of the Nigerian academics. Seen against the backcloth of the solid tradition they spun, they look puny and ridiculous. It is a timely indictment on the academics and the Western-educated African, a theme already encountered in *Old Wines Are Tasty* and *Song of Lawino*. In this instance the balance is tipped against the academics who are mercilessly satirized and exposed to ridicule. It is a provocative play designed to stimulate genuine self-criticism. Any positive response to the play should encourage such debate.

## THE LOVE OF LIFE

It seems appropriate to conclude this survey of Sofola's works by looking at *The Love of Life* which is an admirable summing up of her dramatic interests both in its content and artistry. The dramatist's concerns are explicitly stated in the dialogue. Namely, that the country is rotten, therefore, the radical youths are determined to uproot completely all that is decadent both in the church and in the nation as a whole. They stress the need to clear up the mess made by their parents and to promote a clean start for their own children to inherit. These ideas are enunciated by the Christian youth movement. This small group of young men and women have been offered a Christian Centre through which they can promote their laudable ideals of moral and spiritual decency. But the discovery of the suspicious source of their "great expectations" put them, like Pip, in a catastrophic dilemma as the dialogue indicates:

> Emeka:       This country is too sick for
>              anything good to come from it.
>
> Deji:         We were previously thinking only of
>              a Youth Movement to inject fresh
>              blood into the dead body of the
>              Church, but now the powers that be
>              are asking for a revolution.

Deji explains the central conflict thus:

> The crucial point ... was the most deplorable way
> churches invited questionable characters and non-
> Christians to chair church functions. *The god of
> Naira seems to have replaced the God of the Cross*

> [my italics]. The Council passed a unanimous
> resolution to fight this trend, even if it has to bring
> Student   Christian   Movement   into   a   direct
> confrontation with the powers that be.

Although this statement conveys resolute determination, the group itself is divided because there are some members who are not so militant and who advocate *laisser faire* policy. For example, the Organist says "There is no evil anywhere. We know that some people have dirty money and other have blood money but who are to pass judgment?" Abiodun adds "We must be realistic, no matter the strength of our calling. The Eko Christian Centre is a drama come true. We must say it."

There are two issues facing the group, as Ifeanyi notes whether "to object to the source of funding for the Christian Centre and have nothing at all or to get the money from whatever source and get a complex where the young people of the Christian world will make a point to the unbeliever."

Lola asks "Will the stink of the funding source allow the aura of Christ to reach out beyond its walk?" The organist's reply, "Does the stink of the manure prevent the rose from emitting its perfume?", is leading to a compromise which is averted. The argument concludes that there would have been no need to seek funding from an Alhaji (a Moslem priest) to build a Christian Centre had the wealthy Christians responded generously. In the listing of what they spend their money on we have a serious criticism of the value-system of the Nigerian society. Tolu contends that the church members have money but they spend it "on their four hundred Naira a yard lace attires, on their hundreds of 280 SE automatic Mercedes Benz; on their Murtala[7] spraying shows at parties; on their expensive overseas holidays; on their million naira gold and diamond jewelries a saucer sizes; chains of mansions all over the country. That's where church members spend their monies."

Deji, as the leader of the radical students, argues their case with Dr. Denlola who represents their parents' generation. To Dr. Denlola's question "What do you young people want?" Deji replies, "we want a church that is controlled by the spirit of Christ." The dialogue becomes interesting:

>    Dr. Denlola:    Look here Deji, the Church came to
>                    us from Europe already twisted by
>                    European culture and ways of
>                    looking at life. There is nothing
>                    anyone can do about it now.
>
>    Deji:           Wrong, Sir. The only aspects of
>                    European culture in Christianity are
>                    the style of worship .... The crux of
>                    the matter is the spiritual and moral
>                    death of the church.

Deji's subsequent exposition to his father could be cited as a summary of *What is Wrong With Nigeria* by Chinua Achebe, a book that has no parallel in literature in its forthrightness.

Deji says:

> ... the Church has gradually become so completely
> emasculated that its stench reaches high heavens.
> The Holy Spirit does not exist anymore. and slowly
> but surely the Church has lost a grip of its moral
> sense. It has blossomed into a market place where
> swindling and bitter politicking split the Holy of
> Holies into two .... The citadel of spirituality,
> morality and concern for the well-being of man has
> given way to the destruction of everything noble ....
> We, the young people, say enough is enough and
> we will fight!

Dr. Denlola who has been looking at his son in amazement, warns that "the world out there is vicious" but concedes that "where young people have no vision, the nation perishes![8]

At the end of the play everyone is anxious about Deji's safety and we recall the ominous warning of Dr. Denlola "my son, hold to God's hand. The world out there is vicious."

In the light of Deji's action and the risk he is willing to take, *The Love of Life* can be understood in a more profound sense. It becomes a reenactment of the paradoxical biblical statement that he who loves his life must be prepared to lose it for the sake of the kingdom. Those who accept the status quo, because they are fearful for their lives such as the Organist, must be seen as the destroyers of the nation. Their uncaring attitude throws into bold relief the deep, challenging concerns of Deji and the radical youths. These love life so much that they seek for that life to be meaningful or else it is deemed not worth living. Deji expresses it thus "A society whose youth has lost touch with commitment to the ideals of life is a carcass ...."

*The Love of Life* is a direct challenge to the youth of Nigeria in particular, and the African continent as a whole. Sofola employs the framework of a play within a play for her dramatic statement. The dialogue takes place mostly whilst the youths are engaged in a rehearsal or at a meeting. Obviously Sofola finds this a useful dramatic strategy as she employed it earlier in *The Disturbed peace of Christmas*.

## CONCLUSION

As present, there is no continent in more obvious disarray and none that is poorer than Africa. The politicization of writing that was so obvious in apartheid South Africa is common to the rest of our continent. It is natural that women writers, once neglected, in coming to their own, should establish their strength by focusing on gender issues in education, politics, as well as in art and literature. The dominant perspective in Sofola's writing is the inherent strength of women in their struggle to come to terms with their lives in a society that is still predominantly biased against them. One may argue that most of her plays, at centre, work at the didactic level but this is not at the expense of the literary.

Prescriptive feminist criticism suggests that women's literature should dedicate itself to the forging of a new consciousness of oppression by developing cultural myth of women in struggle and women in revolution. Such an agenda, says O'Callaghan "postulates a female audience and the writer's implicit aim of challenging sexism in language and culture with an ultimate utopian end-a transformed society."[9]

Sofola's plays demonstrate an interest in a transformed society but the writer's method does not adhere to any "prescriptive" mode. Many of her plays feature convincingly portrayed male and female characters. It is true, however, that her female protagonists embody many of the difficulties women face in the African society-problem of inequality, lack of freedom, exploitation, and voicelessness. Protagonists such as Ogwoma and Yetunde are victims of the limitations their society inflicts on them. Female heroines like Queen Omu demonstrates at the other end of the spectrum, the strength and courage characteristic of our fore-mothers, which we, their progenies, revel and glory in.

Sofola's strength resides in her linguistic truthfulness, thematic thoughtfulness, and dramatic thoroughness. She has an unfaltering ear for Nigerian speech patterns and she has ample scope for capturing its rich variety. In our evaluation of these plays if we bear in mind that a play is something enacted, then we can appreciate the sharpness of Sofola's eye for the stage. She is always conscious of what makes a play successful as a performance-the music, the humour, the decor, and the stage directions.

Early in her carrier when, Sofola was asked, "What are you trying to say in your writing?" She replied:

> There are three categories ... from which any creative writer can take his material. It can be strictly traditional. It can be the conflict of cultures. Or it can be strictly, the Western-educated, Western oriented African situation .... Now I write within the three worlds but I deal with problems that I find that are somehow strong in the daily lives of the people.[10]

Throughout her writing life Sofola never deviated from these profound areas that she mapped out as the heartland of her creative activities. It is hoped that Longman will publish a complete collection of her plays. This would be a fitting memorial to this indefatigable fighter and creator, a genuine role model.

## FOOTNOTES

1    Interview with Lee Nichols in Nichols, Lee (ed.).1974. *The Deer and the Hunter's Pearl*. Voice of America.

2    An annual festival of indigenous Ibadan people celebrated to worship theIbadan hills. The festival gives license of expression and the comments usually have bawdy sexual overtones. The devotees of Okebadan are men.

3    Penina Mhando heads the Department of Theatre Arts at the University of Dar-es-Salaam. She has published several plays in Swahili.

4    Adelugba, Dapo. 1978. "Wale Ogunyemi, Zulu Sofola and Ola Rotimi: Three Dramatists in Search of a Language in Ogunba, Oyin and Irele, Abiola; (ed.) *Theatre in Africa*. Ibadan, University Press.

5    See James, Adeola, (ed.) 1990. "In Their Own Voices, African Women Writers Talking," London, James Currey.

6    African Literature Conference, 1982. University of Ibadan.

7    Murtala refers to 20 Nair notes which carry the picture of Murtala Mohamed the charismatic Nigerian leader who was assassinated in 1975.

8    This statement echoes Proverbs 29:18 "Where there is no vision, the people perish."

9    O'Callaghan, E. 1993. *Women Version. Theoretical Approaches to West Indian Fiction by Women*, Macmillan Caribbean.

10    See Interview with Lee Nichols.

# CHAPTER FOUR

## Feminist Consciousness and Young Adult Literature:
## Three Protagonists from the Novels of Helen Ovbiagele
### James S. Etim

> ... no writer, female or male, is a feminist just by writing about
> women. Unless a particular writer commits his or her energies,
> actively, to exposing the sexist tragedy of women's history;
> protesting the ongoing degradation of women; celebrating their
> physical and intellectual capabilities, and above all, unfolding a
> revolutionary vision of the role of women, he or she cannot be
> pronounced a feminist.
>
> (Aidoo in Ogunyemi).

Many African women novelists-Ama Ata Aidoo, Mariama Ba, Buchi
Emecheta, Bessie Head, and Flora Nwapa, for example write about the oppressive
nature of patriarchy in precolonial and post colonial Africa. These women
novelists also point to how tradition, especially polygamy and sexism, has been
used to Oppress women and keep them in bondage.[1] These women novelists are
concerned with depicting "the ongoing degradation of women", what has caused
unhappiness and pain for women and how women can achieve happiness and
ensure their full development and participation in society. In giving voice to
women concerns, they point out what women's life should be.

According to Ohaeto (1996:156), "the revival of female consciousness is...
one of the most significant trends in the development of the African novel." In the
last twenty years, many African women writers have been labeled womanists or
feminists.[2] In her useful analysis, Ogunyemi points out that feminism is
concerned with the following thematic core: "a critical perception of and reaction

to patriarchy, often articulated through the struggle of a victim or rebel who must face a patriarchal institution, sensitivity to the inequities of sexism allied with an acceptance of women and understanding of the choices open to them" (p. 233). She however concludes that most Africana women writers write from a womanist perspective since as pointed out by Perry, they are "committed to the survival and wholeness of the entire people, male or female" (p. 1262). This wholeness accordingly is presented through "positive integrative endings of womanist novels." Ogundipe-Leslie (1996:230) sees feminists as being committed to "a socially just society, wherein a woman can realize herself to her fullest potential, if she so chooses. The right to choose, for me, is the definition of liberation, 'freedom', if you like." In her analysis of African women, Filomina Steady (1981:35-36) sees feminism as "an abnegation of male protection and a determination to be resourceful and reliant." In her very useful study, Davies (1986:9-10) further defines African feminism pointing out that one important characteristic is that of "avenues of choice for women."

Whether womanists or feminists with a small "f" (as Emecheta describes herself, see Ohaeto p.157), both are giving voice to women concerns-challenging patriarchy, interested in showing the inequalities that still exists between men and women and how women can effectively participate in the areas of education, politics, health, and employment to ensure their development. It is in the ending of these novels that the vision differs-womanist novels end with less stridency, celebrating "black roots, the ideals of black life, while giving a balanced presentation of black womanhood" (Ogunyemi: 240).

Apart from Aidoo, Ba, Emecheta, Head, and Nwapa, another woman writer that has been giving voice to women concerns is Helen Ovbiagele. She has written three young adult novels, *Evbu My Love* (1983), *You Never Know* (1982) and *A Fresh Start* (1982), all published as part of the Macmillan Pacesetter Series. This chapter analyses the three novels above showing the feminist consciousness of the three protagonists. We will see strong, highly educated and independent female characters who opt at the end either to remain single or for a more family oriented life. They will rebel and fight against forces that seek to encumber them and weigh them down. We will also see a picture of entrapment which they break free from in order to be fulfilled in their own ways.

Major thematic areas covered by many of the writers mentioned earlier included choice in marriage, polygamy, the importance of boys over girls in the family and how tradition and religion has been used to keep women down.[3] The women protagonists in these novels (see for example *The Bride Price* and *So Long a Letter*) and short stories (see for example Nwapa's *This is Lagos and other Stories*) were constrained in the area of marriage and in most cases had to marry who was chosen. When they deviated from this norm, they had problems in their lives. Ovbiagele continues in the exploration of some of these issues. All her protagonists are introduced as teenagers or young adults. They are concerned with the problems of patriarchy, preference of male over female in education, male adultery and unfaithfulness, and harassment in the workplace. In dealing with and resolving these problems, they are empowered and grow in their feminist consciousness.

In her first story, *Evbu My Love*, Evbu, a girl in her teens, desires to have more education after completing her Primary Six so that she can better her life. She is not satisfied with the life she sees around her since her father, who has little education is a labourer. However, several obstacles are in her way. Her father was in "favour of her getting married right away before she became too old" (4) , the family was not rich enough to send her to school and she was not encouraged by her family to strive higher even though her brothers were studying for the GCE Examinations. Several studies (Etim, in press; King and Hill, 1993 and *United Nations and the Advancement of Women* 1996) show that there are inequities in the education of boys and girls in many parts of Africa. In a patriarchal society, one of the myths is that education does not do much for the girl since she will be married during her teenage years. Clara subscribes to this myth for in advising

Evbu to marry Osaretin instead of seeking to further her education she says to Evbu, "Thu, if you read too much, Evbu, you will have no man to marry you" (6). Evbu rejects this patriarchal way of thinking: that she should be satisfied getting married at a very young age to a relatively old man (her former teacher) and remain uneducated and at home producing children. She has her own agenda-to save money, go abroad and study. "Then I can look after myself when I qualify and not depend on any man." (6) This statement is in keeping with the feminist perspective independence from male control. She rejects the man chosen for her, declaring to her mother "I will marry a man I'm really in love with like you did. Look at the way Papa still cares for you and you for him after all these years." (8) Moreover, she rejects him because she is annoyed at being treated as property and "she felt stifled" at his possessiveness.

Jide Jones seems to provide the perfect escape for her desires and ambition for education and freedom from the constraints of the small town. Apart from his youth and ambitious Spirit, they had so many things in common—"a love for books, romantic and western films, poems, pop music and long walks" (16). when she asks him to spell out the future since at that time she was engaged to Mr. Osaretin, he declares to her, "We could have a really nice time together in Lagos while you wait for me to qualify. You could share a room with Edith, my friend Chuk's girlfriend... You may even decide to further your education while you wait for me" (17). In opening up "a new world for her" (18), she ran away to be with the man of her dreams.

However, patriarchy rears its ugly head again. Jide had other ideas in mind in wanting Evbu:

> ... his immediate burning desire was to bring Evbu to Lagos and have her to himself. It would be nice to show off a non-Lagos girl to his friends... He knew that he had never wanted any other girl so much as he wanted her. Maybe the attraction was because she belonged to someone else, but he was not quite sure. Marriage with Evbu would be out of the question though, because his father had always

> impressed on him that he must choose his bride
> from Abeokuta. Apart from that, he considered
> Evbu's standard of education much too low for him.
> But of course he was not going to tell her that (22).

We also see deception for although he knew he was not going to marry her, his intent was to use her and discard her at the appropriate time.

Even though Jide encouraged Evbu to leave Osaretin and go to Lagos so that they could share a life together, when she gets to Lagos, she is left to fend for herself Jide says to her, "I will pay your share of the rent. I know that's not much, but I am afraid that is all I can afford out of my monthly allowance" (30). Of course this kind of help does not come close to meeting her needs and this pushes her to prostitution. Ovbiagele uses this vignette to show the kinds of problems teenagers get into when they leave the relative safety of the village for the cities. Prostitution can also be viewed from several perspectives including male exploitation and control of the female body (even if it is for a given time period). Initially, Edith finds it hard to convince Evbu to take up prostitution. Evbu is concerned about her reputation and being found out by Jide. Only when she concludes that prostitution was the only way to get money to go to school and better herself and Edith promises to take her to secluded clubs frequented mostly by expatriates does she agree to try it out.

When she completes her education in a Commercial School and takes up her first job, Jide's focus is still in controlling her every move and possessing her body. He begins by saying that her new boss, Chief Odie is actually her sugar daddy and demanding that she leaves her job. She protests declaring "Jide, how can you be so hurtful? You know I love no one else but you" (62). When she refuses to obey his demand, he leaves her in annoyance declaring that he hates stubborn girls. When he leaves, Evbu begins to see the kind of person Jide is:

> Evbu broke down and wept. Jide was always so
> selfish! How could she stay at home without a job,
> waiting for him to hand money to her? Such money
> she was quite sure would be quite small considering

> how thrifty he was! Apart from that it would be
> boring staying at home with nothing to do. Jide did
> not even care whether she lived in a hole or not. He
> had been given a flat by the hospital he worked for,
> but he had not suggested her sharing it with him
> (63).

The young naive girl who left Osaretin for Jide because she loved him begins to see that love is not often a two way street, that Jide is selfish and interested in controlling her and not concerned about her growth. Musa, a friend and a fellow medical student, tries to reason with Jide by telling him that he is too harsh on Evbu, that he is at fault for the way Evbu behaved and that he should forgive her and go ahead and marry her. But Jide would not listen. What Jide represents is a man who does not take the feelings of the woman into consideration. He is out for himself Evbu also begins to see that he may be a big flirt and wonders why he had never asked her hand in marriage even though he was now well off. Their relationship comes to a head when Jide after their visit to a nightclub confronts her about her life. In honesty, she tells him everything. But he is all along interested in her body and keeping her as a possession untouched by others. That is why he is physically violent to her ("he slapped her twice" p. 84) and verbally abusive. And then Evbu confronts him:

> You never intended to marry me in your life, you
> selfish flirt. What about Shade Bayo? She lives in
> your flat, doesn't she? ... What do you know about
> life? I did what I did because I came from a poor
> family and wanted to get educated. You have no
> excuse for luring me from Benin City and then
> ditching me... You've cheated on me with other girls
> too, but I didn't mind.... You are nothing but a
> hypocrite, Jide Jones (84).

After this confrontation, Evbu sees that her well-being and strength lies in continuing to keep a job. It also lies in self-reliance, instead of depending on any man. She gets a new job as secretary to Mrs. Niyi and works very hard to grow professionally. In one of the discussions with Mrs. Niyi, given the fact that she keeps to herself she is accused of being "anti-men and unsociable" (127). She denies this strongly and Mrs. Niyi advises her that marriage is not an end itself "If it comes your way and you are happy, that's good. If it doesn't right now, it will later. Meanwhile, show yourself worthy of being alive" (128). This is the kind of philosophy Nwapa expresses personally (interview with Adeola James, 1990, p.114 and through some of her female characters in *Women are Different*). This is the philosophy Evbu maintains and expresses this to Kemi in a discussion: "... I have matured a lot since Jide and I now know precisely what I want out of life. I want love and happiness. I think I will find it with Steve... If he wants me to marry him, I will not hesitate at all, but I have ceased to hanker after getting married. I only want to be happy" (136). Ovbiagele is trying to destroy the male myth that the primary purpose for a woman is marriage (this same sentiment is expressed by Father Izu in Nwapa's *One is Enough*). Evbu says the primary aim of her life is to be happy and this may be in or without marriage.

In the feminist tradition, Bvbu grows in her understanding of patriarchy and survives the onslaught of male dominance, including the unfaithfulness of Jide. In destroying Jide, the novelist introduces Steve, a more amiable character who is kind, gentle, forgiving and wishes the best for his wife. At the end, we have the celebration of Black roots and the ideals of Black life for we have complete harmony between Evbu and her family and between Steve and Evbu's family and the community:

> Later, he was taken to Isi to be introduced to
> grandma. He and Evbu were taken to the Chief and
> elders of the village who blessed the future union
> between them... When they got back to Benin City...
> there was great rejoicing and dancing that night, and
> the couple was blessed by the elders in the family,
> and were pronounced husband and wife in the
> traditional way (143).

This ending is in line with Alice Walker's idea that a womanist is "a black feminist ... committed to survival and wholeness of entire people, male and female" (1983:xi-xii). In bringing Steve and Evbu together, Ovbiagele retains the feminist leanings of Evbu but at the same time does not allow her feminism to be disruptive of community values.

In *You Never Know*, we have two issues-that of choice in marriage and the woman's growth and redefinition of self after a marriage. Yetunde, the protagonist, wants her way when it comes to marriage. We find opposition coming first from her two friends, Tricia and Tola and later from her father. Tricia and Tola do not like Chibuzor because according to them, he is ugly ("the man looks like a gorilla"), he is not rich enough and therefore will not be able to support Yetunde in the type of lifestyle she is used to and finally, he may have too many relations that all depend on his meager salary. She fends off every accusation and derogatory statement made against Chibuzor by the two friends declaring, "I will still marry him even if my father disapproves" (20). When she is finally tired of their tirades, she retorts, "Close friends or no close friends, please keep your opinions to yourselves. If you really are fond of me, you would be glad for me. It's my life after all. I've this uneasy feeling that you're jealous of my close relationship with Chibuzor" (20). With that, the relationship with her friends end and she is free to go on to face the father. With her father, the mother wades in to help smoothen her path and make the discussion about Chibuzor less confrontational. Alter a meeting over dinner with Chibuzor, her father becomes amendable to their relationship. In a way, Ovbiagele gets back to the theme of the need for young adults to be given the opportunity to decide who to marry instead of the decision being made for them by their parents.

They have a lovely marriage until Chibuzor decides to be unfaithful. A group of men (Abu, Jake and Segun) sit down to discuss their escapades and to behave like it is normal for the man to have affairs. Ovbiagele is attacking this masculine myth for in their discussion, we see that this male behavior only leads to pain and dislocation in families. This is what will eventually happen to

Chibuzor. Indeed, goaded by the discussion, Chibuzor begins to have affairs and when Yetunde is alerted to this, she almost faints to death in finding out that he has been unfaithful. But she is willing to forgive and forget. All this time, Yirika has come into her life and has been pressurizing her to have an affair with him even though he is also married. But she would have none of him. It is only when she is unhappy at the direction of their marriage, when she feels "cheated and trapped" (87) in her relationship with her husband that she finally consents.

Yetunde is unhappy about the direction of their marriage for while she seeks to grow, Chibuzor (after more than 20 years of marriage) is not interested in growing and having a vital relationship. He hated travelling and found going out to parties an ordeal. He was interested in reading, gardening, and going to clubs where he socialized with friends and met women. But Yetunde was looking for another kind of fulfillment with him-travelling, sharing etc. Frustrated, she asked him "What will we do when we're old and grey?... At this rate, we'll be senile in no time for, after all, you're only fifty and I'm still a long way from it" (76). This unhappiness, together with Chibuzor's affairs provide the reason to be for the affair with Yinka.

When Chibuzor discovers the affair, we see patriarchy at its fullest-he judges, condemns, is unforgiving, and metes out immediate punishment. She is asked either to sleep in the guest room or pack out of the house. He threatens to tell the children her story from his perspective if she does not behave according to his orders. He declares, ".... by the time I finish my story they'll never want to have to do anything with you again" (98). We see in this discussion a problem-"her story" told from a male perspective is always twisted and that is why feminists advocate the woman to tell her story. Later, he goes on to freeze their joint bank account even though he knows she has no personal account, depriving her of any money she can use on herself. When she decides to leave because she "cannot live like a stranger in my own home and keep up the pretence that everything is normal between us" (99), he tries to make her feel more guilty: "So, apart from committing adultery, breaking up your home, driving your daughter to suicide, you don't want to provide for your children? Mm, how strange! You're totally selfish, Yetunde" (100). But Yetunde sees through him declaring, "You're cruel, cruel, cruel... Yesterday, I had a roof over my head, today I'm homeless" (100). When she reminds him of his past indiscretions, he pretends he does not know what she is talking about and demands that she leave the house.

When Yetunde leaves the house, we find that Chibuzor really told the children "her story" from his perspective-he told them that Yetunde had a mental breakdown after the incident with Yinka and that is why he had insisted that the children not see her. When Yetunde discovers this, she is upset with Chibuzor and begins to see who he really was. In frustration, she declares to Oghogho "I think your father has overplayed his hand this time... I will never forgive your father for this... I've just realised what a vindictive man he is. He made me suffer unnecessarily and almost ruined the good relationship between me and my children" (108-110).

In leaving her matrimonial home, she gains her freedom. When Chibuzor has a heart attack, she rushes to his side and helps nurse him to health. But he wants them to be together again since "we're sufficiently fond of each other to live together ... and be a complete family" (114). Although she gives serious thought to this, she resolves otherwise when her daughter shows her that since it is her life and since the children will not be home all their lives, she should do what is best for her. She declares finally to Chibuzor, "I simply know that I cannot live with you again and be happy. Pretense would be no use. We'll remain friends of course... " (116)

Yinka also desires to have a long term relationship with Yetunde. But Yetunde would have none of that, deciding more to cherish her freedom. She declares, "No way... It's more fun like this, both of us enjoying a certain amount of freedom" (111). Like Father Izu in Nwapa's *One is Enough*, he assumes that "women always liked to get married as it gave them a sense of security and respectability." when Yetunde finally sets herself free from Chibuzor, Yinka still assumes that they were meant to be together in a marriage relationship. The excerpt below shows this mistake:

> I've been waiting and was prepared to wait a long time for you to come to me... I knew you would come to me for we belong together. You're mine for good. She thought: We belong together? Sure! Yours for good? I don't know about that! I cherish my independence and I intend to hang on to it (116).

She makes a choice, not to remain in a marriage situation since this will limit her potential and freedom. Like Amaka in *One is Enough*, she decides that one marriage is enough for now.

When we first meet Ndidi of *A Fresh Start*, she is 16 years old, just finished her "0" levels and getting ready to go to Britain for her "A" levels. She is so young and naive that she has to be chaperoned to a party by Osifo who is not much older. We also see a girl who has an endearing relationship with the father (she calls him "Popsie"). At age 24, we see her exhibiting many feminist tendencies: willing to stand up for who she believes in-Seju, her husband to be. When her parents continue to object, informing her that she does not even know the parents of Seju, she declares, "I'm not marrying his family, I'm marrying him. It's what he and I feel about each other that matters" (57). Therein lies the clash between traditionalism and feminist thinking-the traditionalists adhering to the status quo in the area of marriage while many feminists believe that the woman should be given to choice to marry whoever she desires. Her mother agrees to the marriage but her father is not enthusiastic about it and will not attend the wedding ceremonies. We see her also willing to share what she has with Seju for she is willing to help pay some of his school fees when his money is not forthcoming. She is willing to listen and have a healthy relationship with him, a marriage of discussion and agreement by consensus. As a feminist, she is concerned about family planning and they agree not to have children until they can comfortably provide for the child.

But patriarchy and tradition will not allow this marriage to survive. when they return to Nigeria, tradition takes over. Seju will listen to his mother who is intent on destroying the marriage, he will behave as a lord (making all the decisions without discussing or listening to the wife) and he will find an excuse to be unfaithful. The excerpt below is illustrative of one of their disagreements, when he decides to act without reference to her (he has been invited to a party in Togo, she expects to go with him and he says no):

> Why not? Must you follow me everywhere like Mary's lamb? Already my friends refer to you as my shadow.... It's embarrassing. What's embarrassing? We've always planned our outings together. It's normal. why should what our friends think affect our relationship? Don't you know your own mind anymore?... I don't actually mind you going off with your friends but you should have had the courtesy of letting me know of your plans. I'm supposed to be your wife, you know. Look here, he said flaring up, I think I've indulged you too much by consulting you about anything I want to do and in taking you out frequently. This is not Europe, you know. You can't dictate to me. You're always trying to wear the trousers in this house. I'm the master here and I'll do precisely what I like. I see. Well, don't expect me to accept the situation. (62)

Ndidi will not accept what he is trying to offer-a life that he is lord, controlling, evasive about his activities and unwilling to discuss issues with her. The clash between tradition and feminist thinking is also brought out again when her mother tries to persuade her to stay with Seju since he provides for her financial security. But the author, driving the point home declares

> Ndidi wanted more than that from a marriage, for after all, she could afford to look after herself comfortably... what she wanted was to be with the man she loved... Although she believed in women's lib, she also believed that the man should be the

boss in the home, but in partnership with the woman
(65).

Tradition means remaining in a loveless marriage, the woman totally dependent
on the man to take care of her and accepting polygamy. However, Ndidi, because
of her education and the fact that she is working can take care of herself. In seeing
marriage as a union of two individuals where each shares ideas, hopes, and
concerns and both work together for the growth of each other, she is in a sense
"committed to the survival and wholeness of the entire people, male or female"
while Oviagele at the same time attacks male excesses represented in Seju. That is
why when she discovers that Seju is having a child with Gbemi, she decides not to
be part of the relationship.

In leaving her marriage, she decides to sink herself to her job. But it is in
her workplace that she will find the highest level of subjugation and degradation.
She is employed at Medegie Electronics, a company owned by Osifo. Even
though she is hardworking, intelligent, honest and has been able to save the
company money through her financial skills, Osifo objects to her being hired in
the first place. We see sexism and gender discrimination when he declares, "... I
cannot work closely with women" (76), "I don't want a female accountant" (77).
When he is informed that she is divorced, he sarcastically retorts, "That's even
worse-the frustrated female" (77). In an attempt to get her dismissed, "he tried as
hard as he could to find flaws in Ndidi's work" deliberately overworked her and
made her work at outrageous hours. Her growth begins when she realises that
Osifo is behaving intentionally and she decides to fight back. She compares her
present situation to how she was when she discovered that Seju had been
unfaithful:

> Why must she always be the one to give in? She
> had given in meekly to Seju when news of Gbemi
> came in. Instead of asserting herself and making
> lots of trouble for all concerned, she had merely
> accepted the situation and Seju had got off lightly ...
> Anyway, the present situation was much easier...

> She was going to stay and only leave the company
> when it suited her (82-83).

She was not going to go away battered and humiliated like she had been in the relationship with Seju. In her professional life, she was not going to allow herself to be pushed around. The confrontation occurs later when he makes one of his impossible demands and in annoyance, she says to him, "You're quite insensitive and you're a slave-driver. I just can't believe that a human being could be so indifferent to other people's welfare... You've never wanted me in this company. The way you overwork me is incredible and I think I've had enough ..." (93). He makes a rather revealing statement during the exchange as he explains why he works her so hard: "... maybe it's because you let me drive you hard. You've never kicked." Therein lies part of the answer on ending harassment in the workplace- "kicking and screaming, instead of lying down quiet." Taking a cue, she goes on to dictate the term of further professional association with him-she will from now on not be overworked and will have her weekends free. He apologizes and begins to treat her with respect and this develops into friendship and eventual marriage.

According to Ogunyemi, "black womanism is a philosophy that celebrates black roots, the ideals of black life... It concerns itself as much with the black sexual power tussle as with the world power structure that subjugates blacks. Its ideal is for black unity where every person has a modicum of power... its aim is the dynamism of wholeness and self-healing" (240). Some aspects of *A Fresh Start* meet this description-the celebration of Black roots where all the members of both families agree to the union of Ndidi and Osifo; Ndidi seeking for the ideal union where she can have power within the marriage institution instead of being dictated to by the husband and there is a positive integrative ending to this novel. The same could be said of *Evbu My Love* where at the end there is a positive integrative ending-the marriage of Evbu to Steve, a celebration of Black roots where Steve and Evbu undertake a traditional wedding before they go through the church wedding, the families acting in unison and comradeship and in this marriage, Ovbiagele is trying to make a connection between Africa and America.

We have in these three novels three strong female protagonists highly educated and independent who fight against subjugation and dehumanization. At the end, they live alone (Yetunde) or in a marriage situation but the spouse is sensitive and appreciative of who they are. They grow up from a certain naivete about life, love, marriage, men, and patriarchy to fight against forces that want to inhibit their progress and subjugate them and deny their humanity. Like other feminist and womanist writers before her, Helen Ovbiagele in her young adult novels is giving voice to the concerns of women today.

## ENDNOTES

1    Buchi Emecheta has argued for polygamy (Sizemore 1996:379) even though many of her novels show the evils of polygamy. For example in *Joys of Motherhood* and *The Bride Price*, there is a lot of family tension and disharmony as a result of polygamy. Aku-nna, one can argue, suffers emotionally as a result of her mother neglecting her in a polygamous union. Nnu-Ego is adversely affected when Adaku is brought into the marriage and there is little peace in the household until Adaku leaves. Indeed, the problem was not only between Nnu-Ego and Adaku, but also between Nnu-Ego's children and Adaku's children.

2    Nwapa in an interview with Abiola James prefers to be labeled a womanist and Emecheta a feminist with the small "f" (see Ezenwa-Ohaeto, 1996:157).

3    Several works can be cited, including Ba's *So Long a Letter* that presents polygamy, choice in marriage and subjugation of women using religion; Emecheta's *Bride Price* and *The Joys of Motherhood* that presents the problems of polygamy, preference of boys over girls in family and the issue of choice in marriage; Nwapa's "This is Lagos" that presents the issue of choice in marriage and Head's "The Lovers" that also presents the same theme.

## REFERENCES

Aidoo, Ama Ata. "Unwelcome Pals and Decorative Slaves-Or Glimpses of Women as Writers and Characters in Contemporary African Literature" in *Medium and Message: Proceedings of the International Conference on African Literature and the English Language*. Calabar, Nigeria: University of Cal abar, 1981, as citedin Ogunyemi, 1993.

Ba, Mariama. 1989. *So Long a Letter*. Portsmouth, N.H: Heinemann.

Davies, Carole Boyce. 1986. "Introduction: Feminist Consciousness and African Literary Criticism" *Ngambika: Studies of Women in African Literature*. Carole Boyce Davies and Anne Adams Graves ed. Trenton, NJ: Africa World Press.

Emecheta, Buchi. 1976. *The Bride Price*. New York: George Braziller.

_____. 1979. *The Joys of Motherhood*. New York: George Braziller.

Etim, James "Women's Education in Nigeria: Improving Trends" *Feminization of Development Processes in     Africa: Historical and Current Perspectives*. Valentine U. James and James Etim ed. Westport, CT: Praeger, in press.

James, Adeola. 1990. *In Their Own Words: African Women Writers Talk*. Portsmouth, N.H: Heinemann.

King, Elizabeth M.and M. Anne Hill ed. *Women's Education in Developing Countries Barriers, Benefits and Policies*. Baltimore: John Hopkins University Press for the World Bank.

Nwapa, Flora. 1992. *One is Enough*. Trenton, N.J: Africa World Press.

_____. 1992. "This is Lagos" in *This is Lagos and Other Short Stories*. Trenton, NJ: Africa World Press.

_____. 1992. *Women are Different*. Trenton, N.J: Africa World Press.

Ogundipe-Leslie, Molara.1994. *Recreating Ourselves: African Women and Critical Transformations* Trenton, N.J: Africa World Press.

Ogunyemi, Chikwenye Okonjo. 1993. "Womanism: The Dynamics of the

Contemporary Black Female Novel in English" *Revising the Word and the World: Essays in Feminist Literary Criticism* ed. Veve A. Clark, Ruth-Ellen B. Joeres, and Madelon Sprengnether. Chicago: U of Chicago P.

Ohaeto, Ezenwa. 1996. "Replacing Myth with Myth: The Feminist Streak in Buchi Emecheta's *Double Yoke"* *Emerging Perspectives on Buchi Emecheta*. Marie Umeh ed. Trenton, NJ: Africa World Press.

Ovbiagele, Helen. 1982. *A Fresh Start*. London: Macmillan (Pacesetter Series).

_____. 1983. *Evbu My Love*. London: Macmillan (Pacesetter Series).

_____. 1982. *You Never Know*. London: Macmillan (Pacesetter Series).

Perry, Allison. 1984. "Meeting With Flora Nwapa" *West Africa*, June 18.

Steady, Filomina. 1981. *The Black Woman Cross-Culturally* Cambridge, MA: Schenckman Publishing.

United Nations. 1996. *The United Nations and the Advancement of Women 1945-1996*. New York: United Nations, 1996.

Walker, Alice. 1983. *In Search of Our Mother's Gardens: Womanist Prose*. San Diego: Harcourt, Brace, Jovanovich.

# CHAPTER FIVE

## The African Response to American Feminism:
## A Reading of Flora Nwapa and Alice Walker
### Francis Ibe Mogu

## ABSTRACT

Feminism as a concept seeks to better the lot of women who are perceived to be sidelined by men in the prevailing scheme of things in the society. It also views issues from the woman's angle. Putting it in other words, feminism alleges that woman as "the other" of man, has (since the genesis of human beings) been at the receiving end of society's injustices such as oppression and suppression. Now, through that movement, a sustained effort is being made to right the perceived injustices. Feminism thus aims to establish or assert equality between men and women in a world which it regards as male-oriented.

The feminist movement or trend has been most vocal in the United States, but its impact has been felt almost everywhere.

This study compares the response of two Black scholars to the concept of feminism as ably manifested in their literary creations. The two scholars, Flora Nwapa from Nigeria (Africa) and Alice Walker from the U.S.A. (America), are avowed feminists who strive to propagate the concept with a "humane face" unlike other scholars and critics who advocate an overthrow of the prevailing dispensation without first of all suggesting a sustaining and pragmatic alternative.

Thus, the study (though strictly with an African focus) explores the concept of feminism from the perspective of Black women in Africa and America. It also criticizes some apparently divisive trends by feminist scholars and critics in their response to a concept whose impact has become virtually universal.

It appears that Black women are now at the forefront of the feminist movement. Increasingly, they have become very vocal on issues that, years ago, would have been viewed as taboo. From the kitchen to the boardroom, they are challenging the status quo and instituting reforms in a bid to provide new models. The women seem to have suddenly discovered a fresh leverage-a new found freedom to express and do things.

African-American women more than any other group, have been behind this trend. By virtue of their living side-by-side with Whites (White women especially) who have espoused feminism for quite a while, in addition to their history of oppression and suppression through slavery and racial discrimination, Black American women have become very vocal and assertive. With this empowerment, they seek to liberate not only themselves from perceived social injustices and deprivations, but also to free other women (especially Black women) in all parts of the world.

In Africa, the response to "American feminism" initially was moot. However, as more and more women embraced western-styled education, their attitudes altered and new hungers were felt within their fold. Old mannerisms bordering on local traditions suddenly ceased to sustain these African women. With time, yawning gaps appeared and old solutions to problems ceased to sustain and, upheavals in social relations ensued as the women began to question everything ranging from their status as housewives and mothers to their roles as providers, servants and midwives. In a nutshell, women perceived that they had been subjected to a lot of unfreedom in the past so they began to assert their independence and resilience.

Feminism as an orientation is not new to African women. From all accounts, it is apparent that Flora Nwapa arrived on the literary scene before Alice Walker, having published her renowned novel, *Efuru* as far back as 1966. But, while Flora Nwapa as an African female, more or less pioneers, Alice Walker situates her efforts amidst a tradition of assertive Black American females who blazed the trail before her. There is for example, Margaret Walker-the author of *Jubilee*, who appeared on the scene before Alice Walker. However, Alice Walker pioneers in another area by initiating a variation of the feminist anesthetics which she subsequent tagged "Womanist Theory."

Both Nwapa and Walker believe and actively advocate the effective application and realization of the full potentials of women in all societies and especially Black women who are seen as oppressed and downtrodden. They believe that since women are equal partners with the men, all efforts should be channeled towards the fruition of such a dream. In all of their writings the two writers express an unflinching commitment to the upliftment of fellow women. They also believe firmly in the equality of women with men and their ability to attain excellence in favorable conditions. Theirs can therefore be described as "responsible feminism."

In *Efuru*, *Idu* and especially *One is Enough*, Flora Nwapa employs her creative talent to blaze the trail of feminism for African women. First of all, contrary to previous fictional works by Nigerian and most Black African writers, Nwapa projects a female protagonist who not only matches males in the society in their endeavors, but excels and actually fends for the menfolk, issuing monetary loans and grants regularly to assuage their plights. In some cases the men are afflicted by occupational disasters (such as very low farm yields, flood, or general incompetence on the part of the farmer). In *Efuru*, the heroine, Efuru grants monetary loans to Nwosu to assist him recover from a farming set-back. However, Nwosu is incompetent and cannot repay the loan to Efuru. He is even too dumb to speak for himself and it is his wife, Nwabata, that rescues him upon their second visit to seek another loan assistance from Efuru:

> Efuru, "we have come to your house. My husband
> and I have come to your house," Nwabata said
> unexpectedly ...

> "I don't know how to begin,"
> Nwabata went on. "We owe you. And we are not
> even able to pay. We thought we could pay part of
> our debt after this harvest, but it was not possible.
> Our harvest was poor. Let me cut a long story short,
> it is planting season again and we have no money to
> buy yams to plant. That is why we have come,
> Efuru, Please help us. There is nobody we can go
> to. You are the only person we can go to. You know
> us well and our nakedness.[1]

Similarly, in *One is Enough*, Nwapa depicts a female protagonist who progresses to the point of nullifying her marriage and charting an independent but industrious life which yields great dividends to not only herself, but to her family and friends. Amaka (the protagonist) thus becomes the modern Efuru who refuses to rot in her husband's house but initiates an alternative that pleases her mother and ultimately yields very great dividends. Like Efuru, Amaka finds it very difficult to become pregnant and give birth to children.

But unlike Efuru who eventually delivers a child while in her initial husband's house, Amaka never puts to bed while in her husband's domicile. It appears that she and Obiora (her husband) are diametrically opposed to each other and cannot jointly make a child. Amaka is presumed barren, more so when Obiora cheats on their marriage and begets two male children out of wedlock. It is later when she has asserted her independence by setting herself up in business that Amaka gives birth, not to a child, but to twins, both of them males!

Thus, the women depicted by Nwapa, like those projected by Walker, increasingly exhibit resilience and independence in their initiatives. Most of all, these women are very humane and humble, showing that even folks (Black female folks) can rise above their peculiar surroundings and limitations to attain excellence. In the process of striving in their societies, the women often excel their male folk to attain fulfillment or self-realization. In fact, owing to their humanity, e.g. their ability to forgive injustices, the women plough back their resources in their societies so as to benefit the less fortunate ones-males and females alike. Generally however, they actively complement the men in sorting out issues entangling their individual and collective consciousness.

In Walker's *Meridian*, a youthful, Black, female protagonist attempts to unravel the mysteries which seem to engulf her and her people (folks) in their Southern U.S.A. society. Racism by Whites on Blacks is at the core of the society shown here. So, Meridian finds herself in a doubly disadvantaged situation-first as a Black person in a predominantly White racist society and then as a woman in a strictly sexist or gendered society. Initially she is naive and illiterate. However, as the novel progresses, the heroine also progresses in her academic attainment-and this becomes her greatest tool for self-empowerment as events unfold.

Walker's perspective here is essentially western just as Nwapa's perspective is African. But their stories are about Black people. Most of the people portrayed are also ordinary Black folks working hard to earn a living.

Meridian Hill embarks on an early marriage in view of her having become pregnant while still in school. She and her boyfriend (later, husband), Eddie are very young and fun experienced about life. So they are full of dreams and expectations-which however, prove elusive. She separates from him and eventually overcomes her academic set-back and goes to college having won sponsorship. Prior to this, she engages in Civil Rights work and becomes more sensitive to the racial situation in her society. This devotion ultimately prepares her for subsequent Civil Rights campaigns while in college and after her graduation.

In her dealings with her friends and colleagues (both male and female), Meridian progressively asserts her individuality or independence. Indeed, eventually, she derives more joy and fulfillment from fellow females since her male friends appear ready only to exploit and abandon her. Eventually, she becomes a rallying point for other folks oppressed by their society. These include males and females (Truman Held and Anne-Marion), Blacks and Whites (Tommy Odds, Lynne Rabinowitz, and Scarlet O'Hara).

Truman tells Meridian:
       "I hate to think of you always alone."
And, Meridian replies:
       "But that is my value", said Meridian.
       "Besides, all the people who are as alone as
I am will one day gather at the river. We will watch
the evening sun go down. And in the darkness may
be we will know the truth."[2]

A recurrent theme in Nwapa's and Walker's fiction is "motherhood." In *Efuru* as in *Meridian* (both named after their protagonists), in *One is Enough* and in *The Color Purple*, the theme of motherhood prevails and the ability of the women to produce and nurture children is the "litmus test" of womanhood in the novels. Thus, women are tainted in one way or the other by their inability to bear and bring up children. Indeed, the accompanying traumas to the women for their inability to bear children is so grave that their whole psychology becomes unbalanced. The presence of children acts as a balm which soothes not only their nerves but prevents them from slipping into mental retardation. Efuru and Amaka become extremely worried and afraid as they patiently wait to get pregnant and procreate. In fact, at some point, their society views them as men since they (as women) are yet to bear children. It is only the birth of their children eventually that brings succour to them- although in Efuru's case her husband, Adizua deserts her and her child (Ogonim) dies, leaving her totally disillusioned.

Similarly, Meridian and Celie dispose of their children to their relations owing to their inability to sustain themselves and the children. However, they are always worried about them. The ultimate thing to do would be to retrieve those children and fend for them. Peace of mind eludes them continually as their children are separated from them.

In *Meridian*, Lynne Rabinowitz is happiest when with her daughter Camara. It is Camara that binds Lynne to her husband, Truman. As soon as Camara dies, Lynne loses both her mental balance and her husband. She subsequently becomes dejected and tries to get succour from her friend, Meridian.

Her husband, Truman equally desires Meridian!

Just as Flora Nwapa in *One is Enough* achieves her vision of full female empowerment through her projection of Amaka who rises from nothing to become something, Alice Walker in *The Color Purple* attains similar status for Black women by her portrayal of Celie and Shug. In an essay, "Alice Walker's women: In Search of Some Peace of Mind," Bettye J. Parker-Smith argues that Walker "lifts Black women off their knees, uses love as a defense mechanism, and raises Black women to a level of royalty,"[3] in *The Color Purple*. She further states that women in Walker's initial novel, *The Third Life of Grange Copeland*, "are cruelly victimized by their men and they move about from day to day exposing their shame to themselves and to their world.[4] She then adds that the situation in *The Color Purple* differs from Walker's previous fiction:

> *The Color Purple* operates on a different plane. It shows Alice Walker's growth as a writer. And, in this masterpiece that exceeds its limits as a work of fiction, she elevates Black women to the height of sovereignty. They wear the royal robe of purple. In her early works, women used their fragile strength to love everybody and anybody except themselves. Now, robed in purple, they receive and accept the right to love themselves and each other. Love of self energizes them to the point that they break their chains of enslavement, change their own worlds, time and Black men. They are prepared to fight-eye for an eye, tooth for a tooth. And they remain women-cry when they need to, laugh when they want to, straighten their hair if they take a notion. They change their economic, political, and moral status, with love.[5]

Parker-Smith thus lends full support to Walker's depiction of Black females who turn lesbians because they cannot succeed in their heterosexual relationships. Celie and Shug mirror this trend in *The Color Purple*. Through Walker's portrayal and Parker-Smith's analysis also, women tend to argue for a return to the Old Testament's Mosaic laws from the New Testament's laws of

Jesus Christ. Therefore, the Bible-and by extension, Creation-is overturned and replaced with a new world dominated by females.

A major observation or point to note in Nwapa's and Walker's fiction is the predominance of effeminate males. They are weak men who do not love or care for their wives but who are brutal and cannot achieve as much as their female folks. Thus, both writers progressively emasculate males and empower females in the societies they depict. However, in spite of this apparent displacement, the women still run finally to the men for anchor and support, knowing that it is impossible to run the world on their own. Adizua in *Efuru* can be likened to Truman in *Meridian*, while Obiora in *One is Enough* can be compared to Mr. _____ (Albert) in *The Color Purple*.

*The Color Purple* and *One is Enough* establish Alice Walker and Flora Nwapa as core feminists in their various societies. More importantly, these novels aptly show their authors' feminist orientations: their characters all emphasize the need for mutual co-existence unlike some shades of feminists that tend to desire a female-only universe. However, though the writers argue for such mutually ordered societies, they tend to argue strongly for a revolutionary reordering of the society to empower women while at the same time disfranchising or emasculating men. This trend is clearly displayed in *The Color Purple* and *One is Enough*.

Mary Helen Washington who has described Alice Walker as an "apologist for Black women," suggesting therefore that Walker "speaks or writes in defense of (the Black woman's cause or position)." believes the "liberation of Black womanhood" is the cause the novelist is vouching for. Washington also feels that Walker "as an apologist ... demonstrates this position basically in the sense of acknowledging."[6]

Both Walker and Nwapa are keen followers of history, especially as it applies to women. Their writings therefore mirror this history vividly. In analyzing Walker's fiction, Bettye J. Parker-Smith argues that:

Historically, Black women have been directed into feelings of guilt about responsibility for the emasculation of the Black male. Guilt, as demonstrated in Walker's women, breeds a weakness that cripples. Women understand that despite the troubles their men see, men are actually able to get along very well together. Their ability to enjoy and maintain a camaraderie is an element of beauty in their strength. Black women not only digest the hurt and pain, they feel it their duty to become a repository of the Black man's rage. This theme is especially paramount in Walker's first two pieces of fiction but is perhaps more openly woven in the fabric of *Third Life*. Black men, by the same token, understanding this weakness and, hence, vulnerability, use Black women as their "punching bag." They are easier to knock out than are the dominant powers ...[7]

Alice Walker, believing that the revision or rewriting of such history was long overdue, set out in *The Color Purple*, female characters who begin to exhibit a different understanding of their hitherto dominant history. In the novel, Walker depicts Black females who resist male aggression to the point that they actually overpower and overwhelm Black males. Harpo is a Black male that marries Sofia- a Black female, and attempts to make her obey him, so he seeks advice from his father, Mr. _____ (Albert):

Harpo want to know what to do to make Sofia mind. He sit out on the porch with Mr. _____. He say, I tell her one thing, she do another. Never do what I say. Always back talk ...
    You ever hit her? Mr. _____ ast.
    Harpo look down at his hands.
Naw Suh, he say low, embarrass.
    Well how you spect to make her mind? Wives is like children. You have to let 'em know who got the upper hand. Nothing can do that better than a good sound beating .
    Next time us see Harpo his face a mess of bruises. His lip cut. One of his eyes shut like a fist. He walk stiff and say his teef ache.[8]

Apparently, Sofia (Harpo's wife) has the upper hand as she overpowers and beats her husband mercilessly. This incident recalls Obiora's and Amaka's "fight" in *One is Enough*, where Amaka, with the aid of a hammer hits and numbs her husband, Obiora, thus overpowering and emasculating him:

> He rushed at her. He was a very strong man. He had beaten her once during their six years of marriage and she did not recover from that beating for a week. Her face was swollen, her head ached. She had bruises all over her. Obiora was sorry and contrite ...
>
> Amaka learnt one thing from that incident and it was that she would never helplessly watch a man, least of all her husband, beat her. She must defend herself. She arrived at this conclusion herself ...
>
> She armed herself with a hammer, and waited ...
>
> Then all of a sudden, without warning, the door was open. Amaka dodged as her husband came after her barehanded. Then she sprang up quickly and landed a heavy blow on her husband's chest with the hammer. He simply sprawled down on the toilet floor, unable even to cry out.[9]

Through such portrayals, Walker and Nwapa categorically state their firm belief that Black women, given the chance, would not only rise to the level of their men, but would match and then overpower or excel them. Interesting as this may sound however, such manifestations in real life are rare and extraordinary. Therefore, such an avowed preoccupation by feminists ultimately could prove counter-productive as it could spur females into greater violent confrontations with males which in turn would make the males more ferocious or aggressive. In real life, the deed beckons much more than the preachment.

Although the emphasis in this essay is on key fictional works by Nwapa and Walker, the personal lives and essays by these two writers further reflect their firm belief in freedom and empowerment for women-especially Black women.

For example, both writers worked very hard to economically empower themselves, overtaking even many of their male colleagues in the process. Therefore they determine their own affairs. They do not believe in wives depending on their husbands for every form of economic support. Such dependence they note, serves to enslave women to men. Nwapa and Walker also had marital problems which ranged from divorce on the one hand, to such related intra-family traumas, and just a child-a daughter to Walker. Both of these writers also draw extensively from their traditional backgrounds to creatively project characters and situations.

Equally illuminating, are essays such as *In Search of Our Mothers' Gardens* and *Living By the Word*, which further anchor Alice Walker's faith in the creative ability of Black women (mothers) and her commitment to nature. Walker believes that most of the current problems afflicting mankind would not exist if mankind properly drew inspiration from nature instead of consistently and progressively destroying it. Hence, it is only in a rural, natural setting that she succeeds in "conjuring" characters and settings for her masterpiece-*The Color Purple*. She admits that her characters preferred a serene, unpolluted, rural environment:

> "What is this tall shit anyway?" they would say.
>     ... all the people in the novel promptly fell silent-I think in awe. Not merely of the city's beauty, but of what they picked up about earth quakes.
>     "It's pretty," they muttered, "but us ain't lost nothing in no place that has earthquakes"...
>     They also didn't like seeing buses, cars, or other people whenever they attempted to look out. "Us don't want to be seeing none of this," they said. "It make us can't think".
>     That was when I knew for sure these were country people.
>     Seeing the sheep, the cattle, and the goats, smelling the apples and the hay, one of my characters, Celie, began, haltingly, to speak ...[10]

Walker extends this admiration of nature to her short story, "Am I Blue?" in *Living By the Word* and to *Horses Make a Landscape Look More Beautiful*.

It is therefore very clear that Alice Walker and Flora Nwapa are pillars and champions of the cause of women's emancipation from the perceived lopsided male-dominated society. Their writings bear lavish testimony to this attestation and there certainly would have been a yawning gap in the American and African settings if these two female writers did not appear on the scene at the time they did.

A major point of divergence between the two artists however, is the prescription of a panacea to some of ills afflicting the females they explore or portray in their writings. Whereas Nwapa falls back on the African ethos to actively advocate heterosexual relationships especially through marriage, with economic independence for both the female and male partners in the union, Walker relies on the American consciousness to suggest lesbianism as an alternative to heterosexual relationships. However, lesbianism (or homosexuality) does not sustain in the long run and is therefore not a good alternative:

> Celie's sexual desire for (fellow) women and her sexual encounter with shug (another female) is never a controversial issue even though it is the catalyst for her resistance to male domination, for her coming to power. Walker makes the powerful suggestion that sexual desire can disrupt and subvert oppressive social structure because it does not necessarily conform to social prescription, yet this realization is undermined by the refusal to acknowledge it as threatening- dangerous.[11] [Brackets added.]

This stance on the part of Walker tends to confirm the notion of the inherent looseness about sexual matters which has debased human relationships to the level of lesbianism and homosexuality in the west-a sharp contrast to the situation in Africa (the so-called dark continent) where heterosexual relationships and decorum regarding sexual issues still largely prevail. In her depiction, Nwapa only depicts men and women who relate sexually to each other. She never projects females who relate sexually to females or males who relate similarly to males. She however portrays females and males who engage in extra-marital sexual relationships. For example, Adizua and Eneberi (Gilbert) in *Efuru* and Obiora in *One is Enough* are culprits in this pastime. Amaka on the other hand, seduces a catholic priest who is sworn to celibacy and chastity, to the point that she conceives and bears twin male children.

Nwapa also creatively depicts an African woman in a modern urban setting who refuses to marry but begets as many as four children. Amaka's sister, Ayo relies on her "boyfriend" who is married with children, to beget children and also to obtain sustenance. Ayo "was not very happy with her permanent secretary boyfriend of late, whose four children she was looking after. It was not his attention that she cared for, it was the money to take care of the children..."[12]

From this brief analysis, it is apparent that women from both sides of the Atlantic share a lot of commonalities as can be discerned from Walker's and Nwapa's experiences and creativity. It is also clear that the women (owing to differing world-views and orientations) have differing attitudes and views of issues paramount in their environments. Generally, the problems may appear to be synonymous, but the women shown in works by the two artists have slightly dissimilar prescriptions for a cure. The level of sophistication of the society involved tends to complicate attempts to proffer enduring and practical panacea to problems.

However, it is beyond any doubt that Black women in Africa and America share a lot of attributes and are teaming up under the umbrella of the feminist movement to voice their experiences, views, hopes, and yearnings for themselves, their fellow females and males and the society at large.

## REFERENCES

1    Flora Nwapa. 1966. *Efuru*. London: Heinemann Educational Books Ltd., p. 170.

2    Alice Walker. 1976. *Meridian*. New York: Pocket Books, p. 220.

3    Mari Evans ed. 1984. *Black Women Writers (1950-1980)-Critical Evaluation*. New York: Anchor Books, Doubleday, p. 480.

4    _____ . p. 483.

5    _____ . p. 483.

6    _____ . p. 480.

7    _____ . p. 481.

8    Alice Walker. 1982. *The Color Purple*. New York: Pocket Books, pp. 37-38.

9    Flora Nwapa. 1981. *One is Enough* Enugu: Tana Press Ltd., pp. 29-33.

10   Mari Evans, ed., p. 454.

11   Henry Louis Gates, Jr. ed. 1990. *Reading Black, Reading Feminist: A Critical Anthology*. New York: Meridian, p. 456.

12   Nwapa, *One is Enough*, p. 115.

# CHAPTER SIX

## Women and Society in Selected Novels
## and Short Stories of Flora Nwapa
## James S. Etim

Novels and short stories are in many cases a reflection of the society or period they were written. Writing along these lines, Ogundipe-Leslie (1994:44) posits that one view of literature is that it "can be said to mirror or reflect society, providing a reliable image of a number of hard, social facts. In this light, literature can be viewed as a social document, a record of ... life in the society ... literature can be used to document social facts and realities in our study of women and society..." Emecheta speaks in the same vein when she says that "every good novel must depict a society. The society is the bone of the story" (as quoted in Boostrom, 1996:58).

Many African women writers are either considered feminists or womanists. According to Ewell (1990) feminist criticism "is rooted in the civic and intellectual unrest of the 1960's" (43) and feminism aims at "exposing male privilege as the primary assumption of the claim to universality" (44). For Carole Boyce Davies "African feminism examines societies for institutions which are of value to women and rejects those which work to their detriment and does not simply import Western women's agendas " (1986:9). Alison Perry (1984) describes Nwapa as a womanist , "a woman who is committed to the survival and wholeness of the entire people, male and female" (1262). Molara Ogundipe-Leslie points out that feminists have posited two major responsibilities for the woman writer "... first to tell about being a woman; secondly, to describe reality from a woman's view, a woman's perspective" (1994:57). Furthermore, she indicates that "Flora Nwapa and Buchi Emecheta wish to educate us about the woman's realm of experience" (65). This chapter examines women's realm of experience as reflected in selected novels and short stories of Flora Nwapa. The analysis specifically will cover such issues as-how does she represent the women in society given the fact that " she was more interested in recording intimately individual women's lives" (Perry 1984), how does she present society that women found themselves and still find themselves, and how does she project the ways women's lives could be and should be? Two novels, *Women are Different* and *One is Enough* and the collection of her short stories, *This is Lagos and other Stories* will form the focus of the discussion in this chapter.

Her novel, *Women are Different*, first published in Nigeria in 1986 reflects aspects of Nigerian society immediately before and right after independence. Rose, Agnes, Dora and Comfort, the four major characters, were members of the first class of entrants to Archdeacon Crowther Memorial Girls School (ACMGS) in January 1945 (3). Miss Hill, the Principal of ACMGS in arguing for the setting up of the school thought that "Nigeria needed well brought up Christian girls who would take their places when they eventually handed power over to the people. Miss Hill could see the handwriting on the wall since the advent of a Nnamdi Azikiwe" (23). Two other important figures in Nigeria's fight for independence are mentioned-Dr. Nwafor Orizu and Mazi Mbonu Ojike, with Mr. Ojike addressing the students on the importance of Igbo culture and language. The events in the novel are situated between 1945 and about 1975.

Reflected in this novel are three categories of women: (1) those who grew up before independence, (2) those who grew up right before independence and a few years thereafter, and (3) children born to women in the second category. A reading shows that women in the first category were greatly influenced by tradition especially that of arranged marriage. Miss Okeke, a teacher at ACMGS best illustrates the case. Although educated, she still fell into the marriage suddenly arranged for her with Dr. Eziso after he had been rejected by Miss Hill. No indication is given on Miss Okeke's attitude to Dr. Eziso or to the question of arranged marriages. We are only told that "Miss Okeke's parents were approached, and they readily agreed that the learned Doctor should marry their daughter" (25). However, this situation is immediately contrasted with the lives of Rose, Comfort and Dora, who represent the second category of women. In the discussion that follows, Rose and Dora believe that they have found their life partners-giving credence to the feminist belief of choice; that the woman should be responsible for choosing her partner instead of being in an arranged marriage. Indeed in the discussion between Miss Onu and the girls, the school encouraged an interaction with boys as a foundation to lasting relationships between the sexes.

The women in the second category raise questions about traditional practices and in many cases, are in opposition to these practices. The conversation between Rose and Comfort is rather instructive in setting the tone:

> "What then is your plan on leaving school?"
> asked Rose.
> "Get a job, work two or three years, hook a man, get
> him to the altar.
> Have two or three children for him, and if he does
> not make it, leave him," said Comfort.
> ...
>
> " You are not going to marry for love then?"
> " Love? I want to marry someone who will take
> care of me. I want to marry a rich man. Love
> my foot." (30)

For Comfort then (and by extension, the "liberated woman"), working for economic independence is very important (more on this later on). Marriage is not for better or worse, not necessarily for love or for a lifetime but for other reasons including money. Marriage itself is not a given for as Comfort sums it "... Agnes will marry her 'uncle' as soon as she is allowed to finish her schooling. As for us, anything can happen as far as marriage is concerned" (pp. 30-31).

Women here also question early marriages which is a staple of the traditional society. According to Boostrom (1996:62), in the traditional setting, "the minimum marriage age for a monogamous marriage for boys was age 14 and for girls age 12." When Agnes (about age 12 or 13 given the fact that she is a first year student in high school) is confronted with the situation, she becomes quieter and very subdued during the term. "She loathed the man but there was nothing she could do on her own ... she was determined to be in school and take the Cambridge School Certificate before she married" (22). Early marriages does not bring joy; Agnes is not happy during her wedding ceremony: "Rose did not like Agnes' wedding dress neither did Agnes who looked so miserable at her wedding day. She could not even smile at Rose when she saw her among the crowd" (52). Thus, the day supposed to be one of joy is turned to sorrow and pain. Even in the consummation of the marriage, Agnes is not happy. In showing us the mind of Agnes, the author lets us see the pain and emptiness in the relationship: "Sleeping with her husband was nothing special. She felt nothing. She submitted herself like a lamb ready for slaughter and prayed that it should be over quickly so she would snatch some sleep" (57). The metaphor here of the lamb led to the slaughter is rather harsh, but this underscores the criticism the writer places on the problem. Early arranged marriages lead to loveless unions that cause affairs and eventual destruction of the marriage.

Women in this category also question the traditional concept that the woman is the man's property. Chris, Dora's husband has that attitude (69) and therefore is unwilling to listen to the wife until she tells him that he will manage the business she intends to set up. However, when Chris cheats her and deserts her and when she meets Tunde, she is not willing to give up her independence and be dictated to again by another man. In confiding in Rose, she shows her dilemma:

> I want a husband not a lover. Here is Tunde, and I
> know in my heart that I cannot stand him ... If I
> agree to marry him, he will start clamping down on

> me and will not give me any breathing space. He
> will start controlling my business, and become
> authoritative (102).

This is why eventually, she will not marry Tunde but will be reunited with Chris when he comes back to her life. This time, however, she has the upper hand for when Rose asks her if Chris has changed, she declares "A good deal. But I have the whip hand. I am not a fool" (133). The situation changes for like the Wife of Bath who takes back power from the fifth husband, she does so at the end.

The women in this category not only question the traditional attitude of not supporting the education of girls but also question the type of education hitherto given to girls. In *A History of Nigerian Education*, Fafunwa points out that in the 1950's and 1960's, many of the girls were provided with education that included Needlework, Home Economics, Craft, Gardening, Health Science etc. This type of education was to ensure that the woman made a good housewife and was often provided in the Modern School. In *Women are Different*, the girls begin by discussing the importance of education for the women and concluding that domestic science is "not education the way we know and understand it" (13). Through Comfort, the author satirizes the view often held by some that it is not necessary to educate a girl since she will eventually marry, have children and forget all that she learned in school. The three girls practice what they preach-Rose and Agnes go on to have a university education while Comfort and Dora become nurses.

Represented in the third category are girls born to the women in the second category. The lives of Elizabeth, the daughter of Agnes and Chinwe, the daughter of Dora as presented are examples of women in this category. Mama Nkem and Mama Emeka at Agnes's wedding give us an indication of how women in this category will behave:

> Rose looked round but there was nobody she
> recognized, so she sat down again and the two
> women continued their yapping.

> "For better or for worse my foot," said Mama
>          Emeka.
> "What do you mean?" asked Mama Nkem.
> "I prefer our own native law and custom marriage.
> 'For better or for worse' Nobody bothers to uphold a
>          marriage if things begin to go wrong."
> "I don't agree with you."
> "I am not asking you to agree with me. It is a fact.
>          Our children will not take what we are
>          taking from our husbands." (54)

Two ideas arise from this dialogue; that women in this category do not look at marriage as a life long commitment and will not take any nonsense from the husband. Chinwe will not stand by while the husband is deceitful and engages in adulterous affairs. She decides to divorce him as a result of his behavior (113-115), marries a second husband almost immediately and gets out in eighteen months when she finds out that the husband is not as rich as he pretended to be. Elizabeth is not too different from Chinwe. Although she is not involved in any divorce, she is part of a mutually arranged marriage:

> Theo then met Zizi in London when she was in
> productive custody, liked her and proposed to her.
> She accepted him. Then Theo told her his
> conditions for marriage. To begin with, he did not
> want to marry anyone. He was too young and he
> wanted to play around. If Elizabeth could leave him
> alone, not bother him in any way after the marriage,
> the London flat which his parents would give him,
> would be her own. Elizabeth agreed, and so the
> wedding ceremony was performed (129).

Chinwe also reflects another characteristic of women in this category-hard work and economic independence. Immediately divorcing her first husband, she started a beer-parlor business. Later, she goes into contracting business, "Like her mother, she was industrious. She closed the beer-parlour and got herself a contract worth one million naira from the new military rulers. She worked hard and was able to finish the job in record time and was paid" (118). Thus at a very young age, she has material success.

In this novel, Nwapa shows that men are morally bankrupt and are partly responsible for the problems of the society-whether in the mismanagement of the political system, in marriages or rearing of children. The new breed of politicians who took over the realm of affairs are described thus:

> The young parliamentarians and the secretaries thought that taking over from the British meant having a license to corrupt young school girls and their mothers.
> There were so many working girls who lived with this brand of people, while their wives lived in the villages. To them independence meant living in the GRA-Government Reservation Area, taking over the positions of the British, driving cars like their colonial masters, but ignoring the grave responsibilities attached to these new positions. The British were not emulated by these new men. The civil service was still regarded as the white man's service, and therefore one could cheat the government and boast about it .... This mentality persisted years after independence and this worried Agnes and some well meaning people like her (63).

The description shows that these new breed of politicians, the new rulers of the country, were both politically and morally corrupt. Corruption has become a bane to many African societies, a cancer slowly eating the fabric of the Nigerian society towards destruction. In Chinua Achebe's *A Man of the People* and Ayi Kwei Armah's *The Beautiful Ones Are not Yet Born*, each author points to the problem and its debilitating effects on society. In *Women are Different* the three girls point out "that the problem of bribery was that there were more people ready to bribe than those ready to receive" (49). Tunde in surveying the situation adds bitingly, "I don't discuss Nigerian Airways or NEPA or P and T or bribery and corruption in Nigeria. It is a waste of time" (135).

Those who are not politicians but worked for the government are shown to be morally bankrupt. Chris, the husband of Dora who worked in the Registry is a representative of the corrupt class for "He was not the only one who took bribes in the Registry. His colleagues and his boss, the Chief Clerk, took bribes as well" (67). When Chris leaves Dora for further studies, we find him abandoning Dora and living with a German lady. The men in the life of Rose do not behave better. After giving Mark her life savings so that he can travel abroad and pursue further studies at Harvard, we find Mark jilting her. Ernest had jilted her earlier and when she meets Olu, the relationship does not go too far because of Olu's wife.

Thus we see that for many of the women, they are victims of male moral corruption. In a patriarchal society, males here are not only morally corrupt but do not take women seriously. The author leaves us with the impression that this misbehavior has caused women to also misbehave. The discussion below between Rose and Dora illustrates the point:

> "Our grandfathers will turn in their graves if they hear of the men who know of their wives' carrying on, and do nothing about it."
> "When the men are equally guilty? Come Dora, this is Nigeria of the seventies, not of the fifties. We must understand, and we must learn fast."
> "If Chris had been faithful, if he had not been cruel. If he had treated me well in Hamburg, I would not have had anything to do with Tunde."
> "I could say that of Ernest too. I think we were oversheltered by the good missionaries. They were good in  their own ways, but they did not prepare us for for the kind of life we would be called upon to live in Nigeria in the seventies" said Rose (100).

In a patriarchal society utterly corrupt, where things do not work and where men are morally bankrupt, how does Nwapa project the ways women's lives could be and should be? In answering this question, the author states:

> Chinwe had done the right thing. Her generation was doing better than her mother's own. Her generation was telling the men, that there are different ways of living one's life fully and

> fruitfully. They are saying that women have
> options. Their lives cannot be ruined because of a
> bad marriage. They have a choice, a choice to set up
> a business of their own, a choice to marry and have
> children, a choice to marry or divorce their
> husbands. Marriage is not THE only way (118-119).

Two ideas emanate from the above—the concept of marriage and the concept of work and economic independence-and I will discuss these below.

## THE CONCEPT OF MARRIAGE

In the traditional society, marriage was a given, the only way both for the man and woman. This marriage, often arranged, was expected to last a lifetime. If it did not work out well, the man merely married a second or third wife. The women were expected to remain in the relationship and make the best out of the situation. Divorce was not an option, especially for the woman. Nwapa, through the characters she develops, is questioning this and asking for a review of this state of affairs for the good of the woman. We find in this novel three generations of women-Miss Onu's generation; the generation of Rose, Comfort, Dora and Agnes; and the latest generation represented by Chinwe and Elizabeth. The first generation represented here lived with arranged marriages but the second generation is that of transition-Agnes begins life with an arranged marriage but divorces the husband when not satisfied with the relationship. Dora chooses Chris and begins life with the man she loves. However, she is greatly disappointed with Chris' behavior and although she divorces him (by native law and custom), she accepts him when he comes back for the sake of the children and because she does not want to be dictated to. Love gives way to common sense and convenience as she declares to Rose :

> ... there is nothing sentimental about having Chris
> back. I am facing reality. I am looking at my
> problem cold-bloodedly, and having arrived at my

> decision, every other consideration pales into
> insignificance ... What is love, Rose? We loved
> when we were in school. After school days, one is
> not influenced in one's action by love, but by
> common sense and convenience (134).

Rose wants to marry but since she cannot find the right man, she is still single. She wants to have children (even without a husband-unheard of in a traditional society) but she wants the right man in order to carry this out. While she waits for the conditions to be right, she continues to work which is one way she can maintain her independence. The third generation will not waste their time on a failed marriage but will move on immediately. Having seen the pain and sorrow in their mothers failing marriages, they do not want to be part of that. As Comfort points to Rose, women of this generation are more savvy:

> What I am trying to put across to you is that I can
> understand Dora's daughter more than you or Dora
> do. Chinwe has learnt a lot from her mother's
> problems. What she is doing is reacting to them.
> Her mother was so good to her father, but see how
> shabbily her mother was treated. What Chinwe is
> trying to say is this, "Mother I cannot take what you
> have taken from father. I am going to have my own
> back. No man is going to hold me to ransom.."
> (117).

## THE CONCEPT OF ECONOMIC INDEPENDENCE

According to Ezeigbo (1996), Igbo women strive for economic independence early. "Traditional or modern, Igbo women, no matter their age, status or condition, espouse dynamic economic ethics. ... By the time they reached middle-age, most Igbo women had become relatively successful or even quite comfortable, depending on their line of trade" (10).

In this novel, we find all the women striving towards economic independence. Dora begins as a nurse and not satisfied with the profession, sets up a baking business that gives her the money to be independent and take care of the family when Chris is not there. Chinwe begins with a beer-parlour business and later wins a one million naira contract. Given her new wealth, she is able to file for divorce from her husband and to declare her independence when she says to her lawyer "No, I don't need his money. I want my children and my peace of mind and freedom" (118).

For those who do not have a trade, education seems the other method to gaining economic independence. Rose and Agnes are highly educated and this enables them to be independent. Dora is enamored with Agnes' success that she plans to emulate her in the way she (Dora) educates her children. She declares:

> No matter what happened, she must give her
> children a good education. They would not be like
> her. Yes like Agnes. She heard about Agnes'
> success through Rose. Agnes had had her children
> and had gone to the university. Agnes was her own
> mistress now. Agnes could do what she liked, and
> there was no one on earth going to stop her (73).

In *Women are Different* reflected life for women principally in the 1950's to the 1970's, *One is Enough* represents evolving life for women especially in the late 1970's and beyond. The Nigeria- Biafra war had ended and Gowon was still in power (to be overthrown towards the end of the story). The oil boom was in place, contracting and corruption from these contracts was the order of the day. Nwapa uses this climate to present some recurring themes in African literature-marriage vs. spinsterhood, motherhood, barrenness, and the limitations of tradition in the development of women. She also tries to destroy some of the myths prevalent in the Nigerian society. One of such myths is the concept held by many that the woman can only be happy in marriage. Izu is allowed to express that concept (and invariably that male point of view) as he states that "he had thought that every woman's ambition was to get married, have children and settle down with the man she loved. Amaka was proving difficult but he would press on" (136). Amaka confronts the issue of marriage head-on when she asks, "Was a

woman nothing because she was unmarried or barren? Was there no other
fulfillment for her? Could she not be happy... just by having men friends who
were not her husbands?" (22). After her ordeal with Obiora and Obiora's mother,
Amaka is not prepared to be unhappy or be married anymore. She equates
marriage with unhappiness and loss of freedom as she declares to Ayo:

> Ayo, I don't want to be a wife anymore... As a wife,
> I am never free, I am a shadow of myself. As a
> wife, I am almost impotent. I am in prison, unable
> to advance in body and soul. Something gets  hold
> of me as a wife and destroys me.
> ... No, I am through with husbands (127).

The metaphor of marriage then is that of imprisonment, of impotence with the
inability to grow and develop physically or mentally. Marriage leads to a wasted
life.

A second myth that the author seeks to destroy is the idea that women
should only have children in marriage. Amaka's mother, in trying to destroy this
myth, declares to her early in the story, "Marriage or no marriage, have children.
Your children will take care of you in your old age. You will be very lonely then
if you don't have children. As a mother, you are fulfilled" (11). Ayo declares to
Amaka "I have four children without a husband and I am happy" (127). However,
in seeking to destroy this myth, the author reaffirms the idea that children bring
respectability to a woman and that women are not satisfied unless and until they
have children.

Amaka's mother represents life in traditional society and what limitations
that kind of society places on the woman. Speaking about her situation to Ayo she
declares that she was part of an arranged marriage which turned out to be
loveless. She declares:

> It is my mother who arranged everything. I
> protested. I said I didn't like him that I didn't want
> to marry him, but she said he was a good man... In
> the first ten years of marriage, I had all of you. But I
> still did not love him... But I remained his wife... I

> would leave home and not return for two weeks. My
> husband did not mind (138).

What then could be the life for the "new woman?" In presenting Amaka, Ayo and Adaobi, Nwapa wishes to show us how fulfillment could come for women. In Amaka and Ayo, we see that fulfillment means children without the dictates of a husband and economic independence. Amaka's mother sums up their situation when she declares "Your sister, Ayo, has passed this stage. She is learning to be like you. She is discovering what it is to be independent. She is discovering what it is to have wealth, she wouldn't sacrifice that for any man..." (118). We see two women who choose what their paths to fulfillment were and went ahead to achieve goals. They are no more victims (like their mother) but could be the victimizers. In Adaobi we see a strong and highly educated woman involved in a caring and loving relationship with the husband who at the same time uses her independence to help the family. She is not a "stay at home mum" but rather with the help of Amaka plans for the rainy day.

In *This is Lagos and Other Stories*, Nwapa continues to address the concepts of choice, the new woman's place in a patriarchal society and how her life could be and should be. The second story in the collection is titled, "This is Lagos." Here, Soha, a primary/elementary school teacher, visiting her aunt, Mama Eze, in Lagos, decides to behave differently from the norm expected of a "village girl." She chooses who to get married to and when this is to occur. In doing this, she gets everyone around surprised and upset. In this amazement tinged with fury, Mama Eze declares to Ibikunke, Soha's husband:

> No...You, you married to my sister's daughter.
> Impossible, You are going to be "un-married". Do
> you hear? Mama Bisi, is this what they do here?
> ... You hear, Mr. Ibikunle, we don't marry like that
> in my home, Mama Eze said. Home people will not
> regard you as married. This is unheard of. And you
> tell me this is what the white people do. So, when
> white people wish to marry, they don't seek the
> consent of their parents, they don't even inform

them (19).

So, here we have Soha who will not be encumbered by tradition-she will marry not only from a different tribe but also she will choose when she marries.

In "Jide's Story," we have women dealing with two kinds of brutalities-male infidelity and physical and mental abuse. Jide is slowly destroying himself and his marriage to Rose by carousing often and having affairs with all kinds of women including prostitutes. Like Dora in *Women are Different* , Rose is  loving, dutiful, and overbearing and is not destroyed (for now) by Jide's infidelity and callous behavior. The reverse is the case for Maria. She becomes insane because of her husband's cruelty and physical abuse:

> Maria's husband locked her up several days in their
> flat in London without food. He beat her and gave
> her no money for her and her children. The cruelty
> went  into her head as Peju said. Before her mother
> came, she was already in the asylum (27).

This insanity, although periodic, is still devastating for Maria and causes her misbehaving at times.

In "The Road to Benin," the theme of the plight of the working mother is presented. Children of some working mothers will get into trouble like Ezeka. There are some similarities between Nwanyimma and Agnes in *Women are Different*. Both are working mothers and have to deal with children caught with or trafficking in illegal drugs. Agnes blames herself and her decision to divorce Elizabeth's father for what has become of Elizabeth. However, part of the fault for Ezeka's  misbehavior can be put on his father who is very permissive and weak.

"The Child Thief" presents the plight of barren women in the Nigerian society. Agnes does not have a child and "she was sad ... she had sadly neglected herself. ... someone else was sharing her husband with her, and there was nothing she could do about it" (51). When her husband decides that she must leave the matrimonial home, her situation becomes more pathetic:

> She moved out with a minimum amount of fuss. It
> seemed as if she had given    up fighting for her
> husband. A year or two ago, she would have raised
> hell. Now it did not matter. She still loved her
> husband, but what could she do if her husband did
> not love her anymore (57).

She decides to do everything possible to get a child when the help of hospitals and
the native doctor cannot solve the problem. She steals a child, claims it is hers and
when she is finally discovered, she is taken to jail. Agnes ends unhappily when
one considers her plight to Amaka's in *One is Enough*.   Agnes could have
considered adoption as the jailers suggest. However, societal pressure that says
that a woman is only complete when she has her children is what the author is
criticizing. Speaking on this, Nwapa says in an interview with Adeola James
about the message in her works:

> I think the message is, and it has always been, that
> whatever happens in a woman's in a woman's life ...
> marriage is not the end of the world; childlessness is
> not the end of everything. You must survive one
> way or the other, and there are a hundred and one
> things to make you happy apart from marriage and
> children (114-115).

In "The Delinquent Adults" we are presented with two independent, strong
willed women who define themselves by what they do. Ozoemena's mother
defined herself earlier when she defied  the traditional concept that a woman must
marry her brother -in law when the husband dies (covered in such stories as
Emecheta's *The Bride Price* and  Ba's *So Long a Letter*). She says to her daughter:

> When my husband died, his people molested me.
> His brother especially molested me. You see we
> were not friends and according to our custom he
> was to marry me. And I resented this. I did not like
> him. Our people said I was a bad woman, but I did
> not heed them. I knew what I wanted. I knew I did
> not want to marry him (71).

Ozoemena defines herself in challenging Azubike, the old man who wants to marry her in exchange for his sending her to college. She says to him:

> Why should you insult me in this way? ... What is my sin? Why do you want to exploit me because I lost my husband, and it would seem, have no means of livelihood. Haven't you a grown-up daughter? Would you like her to be thus treated if she married and lost her husband in a motor accident? (90).

She will not be his property or become an addition to his retinue of wives even though she desires to go back to college to improve her lot.

In this story also, Nwapa presents the lot of women who are exploited or harassed by relatives of the dead husband who feel that the wife had taken the dead husbands money and property for her use (also presented in Ba's *So Long a Letter*). Ozoemena is harassed constantly by Chukwuma's relations who want his money and property, oblivious to the fact that Chukwuma has two children and money would be needed for their upkeep. Even when she shows them the bank statement and they send to collect all of his property in Port Harcourt, they are still suspicious.

In "The Loss of Eze" Nwapa presents another highly educated, strong willed, independent woman who will not be deterred by the loss of a boyfriend.Declaring to herself that "Eze or no Eze, I must live my life fully and usefully" (93), Miss Ezeka goes out, enjoys herself and meets Tunde in a party. Although a relationship is just beginning, we are left with the impression that she can handle herself and make the kinds of decisions necessary to survive in hectic Lagos.

In the selected works analyzed, Nwapa's thesis is that traditional culture places a lot of limitations on the woman while patriarchy encourages her oppression and lack of self-fulfillment. Some of the traditions that do not favor women must be changed or modified or destroyed so that women can be free. She presents strong willed, highly educated, economically independent women who chart out a path for their freedom. If marriage means servitude, they will not marry; if they can find a husband who respects them, they will marry; they will have children but will not be hemmed in in marriage since a woman can have children without the privilege of marriage; they will choose who to marry or go out with and when this fails, they will move on instead of crying over it. With many African countries gaining independence from colonial rule in the 1960's and 1970's and with women's movement of the 1960's, Nwapa in her own way explores how women can be free from the shackles of tradition and patriarchy.

## REFERENCES

Boostrom, Rebecca 1996. "Nigerian Legal Concepts in Buchi Emecheta's *Bride Price*" *Emerging Perspectives on Buchi Emecheta* Marie Umeh ed. Trenton, NJ: Africa World Press.

Davis, Carole Boyce. 1986. "Introduction: Feminist Consciousness and African Literary Tradition" *Ngambika: Studies of Women in African Literature*. Carole Boyce Davis and Anne Adams Graves ed. Trenton, NJ: Africa World Press.

Ezeigbo, Theodora Akachi. 1996. "Tradition and the African Female Writer: The Example of Buchi Emecheta." *Emerging Perspectives on Buchi Emecheta* Marie Umeh ed.

Ewell, Barbara C. 1990. "Empowering Otherness: Feminist Criticism and the Academy" *Reorientations: Critical Theories and Pedagogies*. Bruce Henricksen and Thais E. Morgan ed. Chicago, IL: University of Illinois Press.

Fafunwa, A. Babs. 1974. *A History of Nigerian Education*. London: Allen and Unwin.

Ogunidpe-Leslie, Molara 1994. *Recreating Ourselves: African Women and Critical Transformations*. Trenton, NJ: Africa World Press.

Nwapa, Flora. 1990. Interview in Adeola James *In Their Own Voices: African Women Writers Talk*. Portsmouth, NH: Heinemann

_____. 1992. *One is Enough*. Trenton, NJ: Africa World Press.

_____. 1992. *This is Lagos and Other Stories*. Trenton, NJ: Africa World Press.

_____. 1992. *Women are Different*. Trenton, NJ: Africa World Press.

Perry, Alison. 1984. " Meeting With Flora Nwapa" *West Africa*. June 18.

# CHAPTER SEVEN

## Coramae Richey Mann on Women, Crime, and the Color of American Justice

### Joan Mars

The contributions of African-American criminologist Coramae Richey Mann to the rapidly developing literature in the field of criminal justice span over two decades and consists of several books, book chapters, scholarly articles, and other writings. Central to her work is the theme of inequality and injustice in the criminal justice system and the perpetuation of same by the policy makers who craft it, the personnel who administer it, and the social scientists who continually study it and make recommendations. Mann has meticulously amassed and analyzed the evidence concerning the relationship between race and crime, and the devastating impact of the criminal justice process on the lives of the minority population in America. She is also perhaps the only researcher who has consistently broadened the discussion of crime and justice in America to include its impact on *all* the major distinguishable racial and ethnic minority groups, including subgroups of immigrants who are represented in appreciable numbers in the population, such as Cubans, Vietnamese, and West Indians (Mann 1993).

What Mann has called "A Minority View" (Mann 1993, 1994) pervades her discussions of the criminal justice system and distinguishes her work insofar as it presents the holistic and interpretive perspective that is sorely needed in order to give meaning to the purely statistical, and often erroneous definition of the situation that pervades the literature. In a society that is rapidly becoming more diverse (U.S. Population Census, 1990), there is an ever increasing need for the integration of the unique experiences of culturally diverse groups into the general discussion of all aspects of the criminal justice system. Instead, all too often, especially in introductory criminal justice material intended for college students, the issue of race is either ignored or is confined to very brief and inadequate treatment of the disproportionate numbers of minorities processed by the criminal justice system compared to their representation in the population. Mann skillfully incorporates the discussion of race within the broader discussion of the criminal justice system, analyzing the existing data as well as her own, in order to investigate the experiences of minorities in the criminal justice system.

A humanistic perspective is also a distinguishing feature of Mann's work as she consistently focuses on the problems and pains suffered by those who are processed through the criminal justice system, especially juveniles and women of all races. Inevitably, her writings conclude with recommendations for improvement and suggestions for the fashioning of solutions in the pursuit of social justice. This chapter addresses Mann's contributions on the criminality of women in general and the minority population in particular, and the undeniable relationship between race and justice in America.

## FEMALE CRIMINALITY

Mann's unique contribution to the understanding of the nature and extent of female crime and delinquency lies in her ability to adopt innovative procedures and conduct penetrating analyses of her own empirical data as well as official sources of crime data to support her call for a holistic perspective or what she termed a "unisex approach" toward developing an explanation of crime and delinquency (Mann 1984:268). She expressed the hope that this approach would generate a gender-neutral theory of crime and delinquency through an understanding of the many ways in which the female offender is similar to, rather than different from, her male counterpart. According to Mann, "(a)ny effort to understand the causes of crime must include both sexes, all ages, all classes, and all ethnic groups in the model" (Mann 1984:267).

Beginning with her doctoral dissertation entitled *The Juvenile Female in the Judicial Process* (1976), an observational investigation of the factors relating to differential treatment of the sexes at the disposition stage of the juvenile justice process, Mann's work came at a time when the celebrated work of Lombroso and Ferrero, *The Female Offender* (1920), Thomas' *Sex and Society* (1907) and *The Unadjusted Girl* (1923), and Pollack's *The Criminality of Women* (1950), still defined the dominant perspective of female criminality as being grounded in the uniqueness of the female anatomy, physiology, and psychology. After conducting exhaustive analysis of the plethora of studies and perspectives which followed these works, Mann concludes in her book *Female Crime and Delinquency* (1984), that neither the extent nor the causes of female In criminality have been adequately determined. She attributes this failing mainly to the fragmented and piecemeal approach that has so far been adopted in existing studies, where the emphasis is all too often placed on demonstrating the *differences* between male and female offending, rather than seeking to find the determinants of deviant behavior per se, regardless of the gender of the offender. Mann recommended that extensive research be conducted covering all females under criminal justice processing, including those who have been paroled, in order to create a data base from which meaningful information could be gathered for the purpose of theory building, as well as policy and program development (Mann:1984).

Apart from her work on the deviance of women and girls entitled *Female Crime and Delinquency* (1984), Mann investigated female offending from two main perspectives: minority female offenders, focusing on the double impact of gender and minority status on women who pass through the criminal justice system, and women who have committed criminal homicide, discussing the etiology of female homicide offending in general, and Black female homicide offending in particular.

## THE DEVIANCE OF WOMEN AND GIRLS

*Female Crime and Delinquency* (Mann 1984) provides a comprehensive discussion and interpretive analysis of the nature and extent of female deviance and the processing of female offenders, both juvenile and adult, through the various stages of the criminal justice system. Mann begins by addressing both the limitations of official crime data [the Federal Bureau of Investigation's *Uniform Crime Reports* (UCR)], as well as current methods of analyses, and exposes the myth of the "new" female offender. She conducts comparative analyses between offense classifications within the female offender category in general, between adult and juvenile female offenders in particular, and between subsets of female offenders based on categories representing geographic location (city, suburban, and rural) to reveal patterns and trends in female arrests. The sections on "Theoretical and Conceptual Perspectives of Female Criminality" and "Female Offenders and the Law" (sections two and three) warrant close scrutiny as they set this book apart as a valuable resource for criminal justice educators. In the former section, the efforts of theorists to explain female deviance are detailed chronologically beginning with the work of Lombroso and Ferrero (1920), and ending with the contributions of current criminologists such as Adler (1975), Simon (1975, 1976), Noblit and Burcart (1976), Smart (1979) and Steffensmeier (1980a, 1980b, 1981). The latter section on "Female Offenders and the Law" explores the extent to which the criminal justice system has contributed to separation and divisiveness between the sexes through sexual misconduct statutes which clearly target female offenders, the creation and enforcement of sentencing laws that are gender specific, and the differential application of punishment, resulting in discrimination against both juvenile and adult offenders.

**THEORETICAL AND CONCEPTUAL PERSPECTIVES**

Mann divides theoretical and conceptual perspectives of female criminality into the biological constitutional approaches (Chapter 3), psychogenic approaches (Chapter 4), and the contemporary economic, sociological, and feminist perspectives (Chapter 5). In her discussion of the early biological theories, Mann provides a critical analysis of the masculinity hypothesis which tends to associate female criminality with masculine characteristics resulting from genetic abnormality in the chromosomal structures and resulting hormonal imbalances. It has been argued that female offenders who display masculine physical characteristics may have abnormal "masculine" chromosomal structures which trigger hormonal imbalances thereby predisposing them to aggression and criminal offending. She is careful to point out the importance of gender identity and gender-role identity in determining behavior while demonstrating the inherent fallacy of equating criminality with masculinity (Mann 1984). Her behavioral focus may, however, be in danger of becoming subsumed in the debate concerning the relationship between chromosome structure and the propensity for deviance, as ongoing advances in the mapping of human DNA could only intensify the unseemly haste to find genetic correlates of deviant behavior with reference to both sexes.

Much attention is also paid to research on the impact of the menstrual cycle as a catalyst in the creation of female deviance. This concerns the condition commonly known as premenstrual stress syndrome (PMS) which is associated with the propensity for criminality in some women during the period preceding the monthly menstrual discharge when hormonal changes may produce an elevated amount of anxiety and stress. Mann cautions against the adoption of findings on the influence of menstrual distress without careful scrutiny of the data and methodological procedures on which these findings are based. After pointing out the deficiencies of existing studies, she proposes that social and cultural attitudes to the menstrual cycle in women should also be taken into account. It is worthwhile to note also, that PMS has currently emerged as a possible defense against criminal charges both in Britain, where it was successfully used as a defense to criminal homicide (Binder 1988), and in the United States where it succeeded as a defense to a charge of drunk driving (Scinnafleger 1997).

In her discussion of psychogenic explanations of female criminality, Mann details the tenets of Freudian theory and discusses the works it influenced including the contributions of Pollak (1969), Cowie et. al. (1968), and Riege's cross-cultural study (1972). Mann also discusses empirical attempts to develop psychological typologies of delinquent girls and provides a critique of the Freudian approach to explaining female deviance.

With regard to the contemporary (economic, sociological, and feminist) perspectives on female deviance, Mann's treatment of the controversy concerning the apparent narrowing of gender differences in crime participation deserves special attention. She assesses the validity of the claim that the women's liberation movement has resulted in an increase in female criminality, giving the reader succinct summaries of opposing viewpoints such as those of Simon (1975), Noblit and Burcart (1976), Steffensmeier (1980a), and Smart (1979). She also questions whether official crime data as reported by the Federal Bureau of Investigation's *Uniform Crime Reports,* which reflect steady increases from around the 1970s, in the number of women arrested for violent crime (particularly robbery), property crime (particularly larceny), and even white-collar crime such as embezzlement and forgery, truly reflect an increase in female participation in these crimes. She discusses the impact of improvements in the criminal justice system such as in the area of crime reporting and techniques of apprehension and investigation that may have resulted in higher clearance rates for crimes involving female suspects.

It must also be noted that although official statistics reported in the Federal Bureau of Investigation's *Uniform Crime Reports* (UCR) portray significant increases in arrests for women with reference to both the Part I Index crimes and

Part II offenses, female offenders still account for a relatively small proportion of all reported crimes. Females comprise 51 percent of the population of the United States, but in 1994 for example, they accounted for only 14 percent of all arrests for violent crime and 27 percent of all arrests-for property crime (UCR 1994). Yet, if we look at what the percentages represent in terms of increases in arrests for women as compared to men for the period 1970 to 1994, with regard to the Federal Bureau of Investigation's (FBI) Part I index crimes, we find      that participation in violent crimes by women had actually increased by 282 percent as compared to an increase of 155 percent by males, and in the case of property crime, arrests of women in 1994 represented an increase of 150 percent, as compared to an increase of only 60 percent for men (UCR 1970, 1994). The trend in significant increases in arrests of women is also evident in the case of the FBI's Part II offenses, but arrests of females do not exceed those for males except in the case of prostitution and with regard to runaways (a juvenile status offense). Despite the rapidly increasing rates of female offending, the overall male-female ratio for arrests, according to UCR data, is about four to one, and males still account for the overwhelming majority of crimes committed in the United States.

## FEMALE OFFENDERS AND THE LAW

Mann's observations with regard the enforcement of the laws against female offenders is also worthy of special attention. Adopting a historical approach, Mann demonstrates how the concerns of a predominantly male criminal justice administration, concerning the enforcement of public morals and the adherence of females to their assigned societal roles, have influenced the discriminatory treatment of females through all stages of the criminal justice process. The adoption and use of sentencing statutes which would permit longer periods of "rehabilitation" for females, the aggressive prosecution of girls suspected of sexual misconduct as well as the differential enforcement of laws targeting adult sexual deviance, are all explored to reveal what Mann calls the "double standard of the law" (Mann 1984:118). Piecemeal attempts of state supreme courts to address the problems of gender-specific sentencing statutes, which result in longer sentences for women convicted of the same offenses as men, are discussed with reference to Connecticut, Pennsylvania, and New Jersey.

Mann also provides evidence of what she calls "paternalism" and "chivalry" from the gatekeepers of the criminal justice system through the differential exercise of discretion, and demonstrates how the anxiety to "protect" young girls while enforcing public morals, results in the distortion of the philosophy of juvenile justice. This section also includes a discussion of the alleged changes in the treatment of females by law enforcement personnel that reflect the struggle for equality waged by the women's liberation movement. However, as Mann points out, the unique experiences of humiliation and degradation experienced by women because of their gender still remain, as for example, the practice of carrying out intrusive body searches of female suspects who are taken into the custody by police.

A useful discussion of the history of the involvement of women as operatives in the criminal justice system fulfilling the role of police officers concludes this section. Mann discusses several studies that investigated the nature of a policewoman's work, the challenges she faces, and her effectiveness in the police role, and identifies the many positive results that accrue to society from the involvement of women in the law enforcement function.

Apart from the sections highlighted above, this book also presents evidence of the unequal treatment of juvenile and adult females in the judicial process, and provides a detailed account of the historical development of the juvenile justice system and process. A discussion of the corrections system, the pains of imprisonment for females and their dependents, as well as the challenges facing women on death row, completes this treatise on female crime and delinquency in America.

Mann's work on the deviance of women and girls and the processing of females through all stages of the criminal justice system is an informative and critical analysis of the reality of crime and justice for females. Her constant comparisons of the differential treatment afforded to females as compared to males allows for an understanding of the importance of gender in determining the nature and extent of criminal justice processing, especially for juveniles. Her call for a "unisex" approach to theory building is grounded in the evidence she has presented and the analyses conducted to show the adverse results of fragmentation and separation, evidence which also supports her concluding proposal that until we can accurately *define and understand* the magnitude of the problems faced by females, it is futile to engage in speculation as to the causes.

Mann proposes a wide array of changes that are urgently needed for the amelioration of the condition of women in the system. These include policy and program improvements, human relations and sensitivity training for law enforcement officers and changes in the laws, practices, and procedures which govern the judicial and corrections systems. Mann called these changes "removing the blindfold from justice" for the creation of a "nonsexist, nonclassist, nonracist, and just society" (Mann 1984: 271).

## MINORITY FEMALE OFFENDERS

The discussion of the fate of minority female offenders in the criminal justice system forms part of the larger body of work that Mann has authored on the subject of minorities and the criminal justice system. Her research with regard to female offenders in particular, focuses on the processing of African-American/Black, Hispanic/Latina including Puerto Rican and Cuban, Native American, and Asian American women as far as the data would allow, through all stages of the criminal justice process from arrest to incarceration (Mann 1989, 1995a). She identifies violent crime, alcohol related and drug related offenses, and prostitution as accounting for the majority of the arrests of minority women (Mann 1989, 1995a). Official statistics indicate that arrests of women in general as a single group, have spiraled in recent years. As stated earlier, arrests of females for violent crime (murder, forcible rape, robbery, and aggravated assault) increased by as twice as much as males for the period 1970 to 1994. Liquor law violations by women increased by 222 percent as compared to 104 percent for men during the same period. Drug related offenses committed by women include larceny, burglary, fraud, and embezzlement as well as crimes directly related to drug use such as possession, trafficking, and selling drugs. The rate of arrests of females for these offenses followed a similar pattern, increasing by over 160 percent in the case of embezzlement, and 217 percent in the case of drug abuse, between 1970 and 1994 (UCR 1970, 1994). In 1994 alone, women accounted for 33.3 percent of all arrests for larceny-theft, 39 percent of all arrests for fraud, 41 percent of all arrests for embezzlement, and 10.4 percent of all arrests for burglary. However, with regard to prostitution and commercialized vice, arrests of all women actually decreased by 19.2 percent between 1985 and 1994 (UCR 1985, 1994).

What Mann contributes to the discussion of these patterns in female offending that distinguishes her work, is the meticulous analyses of official statistics to identify trends and patterns in the nature and frequency of the offending of women of color as a general group, and each individual minority group as an independent entity in its own right. She also compares the offending of these groups with the offending of White women. In her analysis of 1990 UCR arrest data for New York, Florida, and California, Mann found that while alcohol and drug-related crimes characterized the offending of White women, African-American women were most often arrested for drug offenses and prostitution, Hispanic women for drug offenses, Native-American women for alcohol-related offenses and Asian women for property offenses (Mann 1995a) Mann also rank-ordered arrests for the FBI Part I Index crimes as well as a host of Part II offenses to provide a variety of detail on the arrests of minority women in the three states she examined. Mann reveals how little the patterns in the arrest of women in general, and minority women in particular, have changed and explains the disproportionate number of arrests for prostitution with regard to African-American women and to a lesser extent Hispanic women both in terms of the hazards of "street walking," as well as the differential exercise of police discretion to arrest (Mann 1989).

Mann discusses several studies, including her own research, which reveal a pattern of differential treatment of minority women at key decision-making points in the criminal justice process. She points out that in the case of African-American women in particular, punishment is received not only for their crime but also for their double minority status represented by gender and ethnicity. Study findings relating to the first key decision in the criminal justice process, whether or not pretrial release is obtained, suggests that several forces may be combining to produce an unfavorable result in the case of minority women. Mann (1989) cites factors such as the traditionally harsh treatment that is usually meted out to women who continually offend public morality (such as prostitutes) and are often unable to make the high bail payments set by judges in order to obtain their release. Since minority, and especially African-American women, comprise the majority of those arrested for this offense, it can translate into an apparent disparity. The effect of economic factors such as the inability to retain a private defense attorney, as well as racial prejudice on the part of individual judges can all combine to produce vast disparities in the number of minority as opposed to White women who fail to obtain release from detention pending the outcome of their cases.

The fact that racial bias can influence the exercise of prosecutorial discretion has been suggested in study findings discussed by Mann (1995a), but it is in the area of differential conviction and sentencing patterns, according to race, where Mann has been able to amass the most voluminous and convincing evidence. Official statistics analyzed by Mann illustrate the overwhelmingly disproportionate representation of minority women in the prison population compared to their percentage in the general population. The situation as Mann described it in 1990 remains largely the same today with minority women, especially African-Americans being the most populous in the female prison population both at the state and federal levels. Mann supports her conclusion that minority women, especially African-Americans and Hispanics, are more likely to be imprisoned for their crimes, and for longer periods of time than White women, with comparisons of arrest and sentencing rates in Florida, California, and New York which reveal disproportionate conviction and incarceration rates for minority women with reference to violent offenses, drug violations, and property offenses (Mann 1995a). She also presents corroborative findings of studies conducted by others, including studies which found that African-American women served longer periods of their sentences in prison. Additionally, African-American women were also disproportionately represented on the nation's death rows, compared to their representation in the general population.

Mann identified the rural locations of women's prisons and their predominantly White staff as further exacerbating the race-related problems of minority offenders. She cites the results of a study conducted by Kruttschnitt (1983) as follows:

> A majority of both white and nonwhite (African American and Native American) female inmates in a study of the Minnesota Correctional Institution for Women, (MCIW), where 93 percent of the staff and administration were white, felt that racial/ethnic status influenced the way correctional officers treated female inmates. Racial discrimination was perceived by over two-thirds of the women of color, and 29.4 percent felt that job assignments in the institution were influenced by race. Women of color, who constituted 42 percent of the MCIW prison population, cited "race relations" as the most frequent cause of intra-inmate assaults." (Mann 1995a: 130).

According to Mann, among other problems relating to the location of prisons are difficulties in obtaining access to the parole board, and the negative impact on family visitation, and education and training opportunities. Mann also discusses the language barrier faced by Hispanic women who are not permitted to speak, read, or write in their native language while in prison.

Mann repeated her call for a survey of all female inmates in the country in order to "provide a sound, empirical basis for policy changes that could ameliorate the status and condition of arrested, incarcerated, probationed, and paroled minority female offenders in this nation" (Mann 1989:106). Focusing on the differential exercise of police discretion at the arrest stage of the criminal justice process, she emphasized the need for culture, race, gender, and community relations training for law enforcement personnel.

Mann's findings with regard to the likelihood that minority female defendants will be detained prior to trial, are particularly troubling because of the inevitable "spillover" effect of pretrial detention on the probability of incarceration and generally harsher sentences following conviction. Mann suggests that minority women should be released, as often as circumstances permit, on their own recognizance, since the majority of these women are heads of households, and in addition, are without the economic resources to secure their release, even if bail is granted. Statistics released by the U.S. Department of Justice (1991) show that more than 76 percent of the women in prison are mothers and about 88 percent of these mothers indicated that one or more of their children were under the age of 18 years (Greenfield et. al. 1991). Nearly four out of five of these incarcerated mothers with children had lived with their children before entering the prison (Greenfield et. al. 1991). Separation from children, especially for women who are single parents, is a burden of imprisonment that is borne not only by the parties involved, but eventually by society as a whole, as these children are usually channeled into foster care and eventually manifest the negative effects of family disintegration.

Mann appeals for measures to prevent the severance of family ties in the recommendations she makes for the improvement in the treatment of minority women confined in the nation's correctional facilities. Noting the resilience of the corrections system to movements for change and improvement, Mann states her case as follows:

> Every effort should be made to maintain and strengthen the fragile family ties of minority woman offenders incarcerated in jails and prisons through widened avenues of communication, more home furloughs, conjugal visits, and family life and child care educational programs. Pregnant inmates should be permitted to keep new-born infants while in prison to enhance the bonding process. Legal services, law libraries, and access to courts should be afforded to all women in prison to assist them in preparing defenses and appeals and to properly deal with legal problems concerning their children (Mann 1989: 107).

Other changes proposed by Mann for the improvement of the treatment of minority women in the criminal justice process include the elimination of indeterminate sentencing in order to remove the disparities it perpetuates in the punishment and sentencing of minority women as compared to White women and the decriminalization of prostitution, drug and alcohol abuse, and other victimless crimes. She proposes that chemical addiction and alcohol abuse should be treated primarily as health problems for those afflicted therewith, rather than a criminal justice issue.

Mann also identifies the need for the dissemination of information regarding the system of Native-American tribal law and justice, and the provision of translators for non-English speaking minorities who are processed by the criminal justice system. She recommends that the representation of minorities and women be increased among those responsible for decision-making in the administration of justice such as judges, administrators, and parole officers. There is some evidence that the appointment of African-American judges has helped to ameliorate the effect of racial bias as a determinative factor in sentencing disparity both at the state and federal levels (Walker et. al. 1996).

Mann's work on the "double jeopardy" of minority women in the criminal justice system covers the impact of race and gender discrimination at every stage in the process. She points out the disparities in the criminal justice system with reference to minority women, and presents evidence to support her conclusion that in many instances the disparities are a result of discrimination against women of color by the operatives of the criminal justice system. Mann also introduces the concept of "institutional racism," a phenomenon which is both insidious and pervasive in its negative effects on minorities in the criminal justice system (Mann 1989:107). This term is used to describe a situation whereby racial discrimination results from the application of established and entrenched criminal justice rules and policies that produce racial effects. Mann elaborates and expands on this theme in her work on minorities in general, which will be discussed later in the chapter.

## THE ETIOLOGY OF FEMALE HOMICIDE

Apart from her work on the deviance of women and girls and the special challenges faced by minority women, Mann's contributions on women offenders includes a comprehensive investigation of women who have committed criminal homicide. In her book *When Women Kill* (1996), Mann reviews existing studies on female homicide offenders and presents the findings of an exploratory study which was conducted in 1985 and 1986 in six United States cities (Atlanta, Georgia; Baltimore, Maryland; Chicago, Illinois; Houston, Texas; Los Angeles, California; and New York City, New York). These cities were identified as having homicide rates that were equal to, or greater than, the national rates for both of the study years that were chosen, 1979 and 1983. Mann's distinguishing holistic and humanistic perspective is again demonstrated in this work as she states her task to be not only the investigation of the motives and modus operandi of female homicide offenders but also the furtherance of an understanding of homicidal violence in general and the "necessity of regarding the problem of violence as a human, not just a gender, issue" (Mann 1996:19).

In essence, Mann's profile of today's typical female homicide offender ("a single, thirty-one-year-old, unemployed African-American mother with less than a high school education who has been arrested in the past" (Mann 1996:164)), bears several similarities to today's typical male homicide offender: African-American, with a history of prior arrests or convictions and an average age of 32 years (Dawson et. al. 1993). Mann adopts a study approach which utilizes detailed descriptive analyses of the circumstances surrounding the murders, characteristics and motives of the offenders, and the criminal justice processing of their cases from arrest through sentencing. Mann's contributions on female-perpetrated homicides come at a time when homicide rates indicate that there is need for research that can lead to a better understanding of the social production of homicidal violence *in general.* The homicide rate (deaths per 100,000 population) for the United States during the period 1989-90 was 9.6, which is three (3) to 20 times the rate of other developed countries such as the United Kingdom, Japan, Denmark, Switzerland, Austria, Portugal, Canada, Hungary, and Scotland (Fingerhut 1993). The U.S. homicide rate for women was 4.1 per 100,000 population, which was higher than in all the other developed countries mentioned. Since 1994, when a five percent (5%) decrease in the national murder rate over the previous year was reported (UCR 1993, 1994) it appears that homicide rates may be stabilizing somewhat, although the actual number of persons killed this way-an estimated 20,000 each year (Senna and Siegel 1996:59)-is still unacceptably high.

According to Mann, the choice of cities as the unit of analysis in the exploratory study which forms the basis of her book *When Women Kill,* despite the disadvantage of the limitations placed thereby on the generalizability of findings, was dictated by the availability of "rich" sources of information at this level (such as police homicide files). Mann uses three analytic strategies to interpret the data she collected and in so doing provided a classic illustration of the use of mainly qualitative methods in the design and conduct of social research. Coupled with the meticulous explanations and cohesive organization of the material, this book expands and clarifies existing knowledge on female homicide offending as well as provides instructive reading for students of research methods.

Several similarities between female-perpetrated homicide and homicide in general emerged from Mann's findings. These were to be found mainly in the area of victim and defendant characteristics, and the role played by interpersonal conflict, drugs and/or alcohol in the production of criminal homicide. With regard to victim and defendant characteristics, Mann found that African- Americans were disproportionately represented both as offenders and as victims in the cities she studied. Data revealed by the Bureau of Justice statistics in its report entitled *Murder in Large Urban Counties, 1988* indicate that in the nation's 75 most populous counties, African-Americans comprised 62 percent of all murder defendants and 54 percent of all murder victims, figures that were several times larger than the percentage of Black residents in the general population in the counties sampled (20 percent) (Dawson et. al. 1993).

Another similarity between the victim and defendant characteristics identified by Mann and those reported in the national sample, was that murder offenders and their victims tended to be of the same race and ethnicity. In Mann's study, 93.5 percent of the victims of Black homicide offenders and 92.4 percent of non-Black defendants were of the same race. In the national analysis of murder in large urban counties referred to herein, almost all Black victims (94 percent) and three-fourths of White victims (76 percent) were killed by persons of their own race, and overall 80 percent of all defendants had a victim of the same racial background (Dawson et. al. 1993). Similarly, in both studies, most of the victims of the homicides were adult males, their killers acting alone and inflicting the fatal injury with guns or knives about 80 percent of the time.

More than half of the female killers researched by Mann, and three-quarters of the national sample had been arrested and/or convicted prior to the homicide. With regard to the victim-offender relationship Mann found that the victims of female killers were often intimates (spouses, lovers, relatives), friends or acquaintances rather than strangers. In the national survey about 8 in 10 victims of criminal homicide were killed by someone with whom they were living, or by relatives, or acquaintances (Dawson et. al. 1993). This follows a historical pattern whereby most murders tend to involve victims and offenders who had a prior relationship with each other, but a reversal in this trend began to occur in 1992, when official statistics revealed that 53 percent of the murders that had been committed nationwide involved victims and offenders who were strangers to each other (UCR 1993).

The existence of interpersonal conflict at the time of the murders, which could be inferred from Mann's results regarding the presence of *victim-precipitation*,[1] in 65.7 percent of the cases studied; also bears similarity to findings at the national level where personal conflict was followed by the criminal homicide in 44 percent of the cases studied (Dawson et. al. 1993). Mann also considered the possibility of murder resulting from what is known as *battered woman syndrome*,[2] but ruled it out as a possible explanation in the cases she examined.

With regard to the role of drugs/alcohol as a factor contributing to the homicide offending of women, Mann found that alcohol rather than drug use, both on the part of victims and offenders, had preceded the murders in more than one third of the cases. Although information on drug use in the national sample of homicide offenders was not available, about 12 percent of the victims were engaged in a drug relationship with their killers, and 18 percent of the offenders committed the homicide in connection with a crime involving illegal drugs. In a subsequent survey of murder cases disposed of in 1988 in the courts of large urban counties in the United States, Dawson and Langan (1994) found that 64.4 percent of defendants and 47.4 percent of all victims had been using alcohol at the time of the murder. In 1986, slightly more than one third of state prison inmates admitted to being under the influence of some type of illegal drug[3] at the time of the commission of the offense for which they were currently incarcerated (Greenfield et. al. 1991). These comparisons show that female homicide offending is more similar than different from homicide offending in general and that there is much to be learned from the type of approach which, as Mann suggests, would treat homicide as a human problem.

Other findings of special interest by Mann include those relating to the effect of race/ethnicity on the processing and sentencing of female homicide offenders and variations between cities in the treatment awarded to women. Mann found no conclusive evidence of more punitive treatment for non-White women, although they tended to receive the most serious charge[4] for their crime. Differences were however apparent in the criminal justice processing between the cities studied. In cities located in the Southern states such as Atlanta, Georgia and Houston, Texas, where murder is more common, more serious charges and harsher sentences tended to be imposed.

There is no doubt that the solemnity of the justice process for the most serious offense of murder, substantially limits the circumstances under which pro secutorial discretion may be exercised and leaves little opportunity for the exercise of police discretion. This in itself tends to level the playing field for all defendants who, provided that they are identified as suspects by the police, and there is sufficient probable cause, will most likely be prosecuted for some degree of criminal homicide. The gravity of the crime of murder severely limits the exercise of discretion at this stage of the proceedings, except as to the seriousness of the charge that will be brought. Mann's finding of differences in the treatment of White as compared to non-White female offenders at this stage of the proceeding is therefore not surprising. Another significant point where the exercise of discretion is severely limited by the gravity of the offense is the judicial decision as to whether pretrial release will be granted, and if so, the amount of the bail bond. For example, bail is hardly ever granted in cases of first degree murder with aggravating circumstances, regardless of the gender, race/ethnicity or socioeconomic status of the defendant.

Although in many cases of this type, there is still room for the exercise of judicial discretion at the time of sentencing, Mann found that minority, and especially African-American women, tended to receive similar sentences as did White women, and in some cases were even treated more leniently (Mann 1990a). This was surprising and inconsistent with earlier findings of harsher treatment being accorded to minorities at every stage of the criminal justice process, including the sentencing stage wherever statutes allowed for the exercise of judicial discretion. Apart from Mann's work, research studies on the Black female offender vis-a-vis the White female offender (Wolgang 1958, Adler 1975, Simon 1975, French 1977, 1978, McClain 1982), and the convergence-divergence debate with regard to Black/White rates of female offending (Laub et. al. 1985), have not revealed any features of criminal justice processing by crime type that seem to reverse patterns of differential treatment generally experienced by minority women, particularly those of African descent. Further empirical investigation of atypical findings such as these may shed new light on this vexed question of the dispensation of unequal justice.

Mann also investigated the applicability of the "subculture of violence"[5] theory to African-American women but found no support for it. Instead, she identified a "subculture of hopelessness" (Mann 1990a: 198) that characterizes the lives of Black women homicide offenders and is closely related to their constant struggle for economic survival. This finding is in keeping with those of Hill and Crawford (1990) who identified structural variables such as unemployment rates and socioeconomic status as the primary predictors of Black female criminality. Mann suggests that more research attention should be directed to the study of the homicide offending of African-American females who, as a group, are disproportionately represented in frequency of arrests for murder and non-negligent homicide (Mann 1990).

Apart from disproportionate arrest rates for murder, however, the most troubling question with regard to African-American women is their *uniquely high rates of homicide* (deaths per 100,000 population). According to mortality statistics[6] released by the National Center for health Statistics (NCHS), in 1990 the age-adjusted (15-24 years) homicide rate for Black females was 13.0 per 100,000 population (Fingerhut 1993). This figure was close to five times that for White females, which was 2.8 per 100,000 population. The rate for Black females ranked second only to the astounding rate for Black males, which at 68.7 per 100,000 population, was nearly eight times the rate for White males (8.9 per 100,000 population). Currently, despite the slight reduction in murder rates at the national level, there appears to be no evidence of convergence in homicide rates between Black and White females. Mann's call for more attention to be devoted to understanding and reducing homicide is one that should be taken very seriously, especially by the minority community.

Mann's analyses of the etiology of female homicide in the United States is well documented, thoughtful, and thought provoking. It forms a major part of her contributions on women and crime. The remainder of this chapter will focus on the more controversial aspect of Mann's contributions in the field of criminal justice-her writings on the relationship between race and justice in America.

## THE COLOR OF AMERICAN JUSTICE

No stranger to the effects of race prejudice and discrimination in her own personal life (Mann 1995b), Mann's position on the relationship between race and crime in America has been thoroughly researched, meticulously presented and vigorously defended (Mann 1990b, 1993, 1994). Although not the first to conceptualize American justice in the context of color, she certainly deserves credit for popularizing this concept, which is now acknowledged as a useful way of approaching the discussion of crime and justice in America (Walker et. al. 1996). Apart from compiling comprehensive evidence of racial discrimination in the criminal justice system, Mann has taken the lead among female criminologists in responding, both in writing and in public discussions and debates (Mann 1990b), to the controversial "no discrimination thesis" advanced by Wilbanks (1987). This thesis relegates to the realm of pure mythology, the argument that the criminal justice system is racist, and has been the center of heated controversy among criminal justice researchers for several years (MacLean et al. 1990a).

Mann's contributions on the subject of race and justice in America demonstrates the importance of the inclusion of the minority perspective in the rapidly increasing literature on the criminal justice system. She consistently calls for extensive studies to be undertaken in order to promote (a) sound theory building and program development, (b) more productive ways of creating awareness, understanding and tolerance for the racial and cultural diversity, (c) the amelioration of the condition of minority women, and juveniles in particular, throughout all stages of criminal justice processing, and (d) the reversal of negative criminal justice policies, such as current initiatives that put a premium on the warehousing of minorities (Mann 1993). Mann's contributions on the impact of race also underscore the urgent need for the participation of minority, and especially African-American scholars, in the fashioning of solutions for the current crises in the administration of justice.

Characterizing the disproportionate involvement of minorities in crime as an adaptive response to structural inequality, economic deprivation and race and class oppression, Mann utilizes the conflict perspective in criminology that is associated with the work of Quinney (1970) and Chambliss and Seidman (1971). Evidence is meticulously presented to support her claim that the criminal justice system, as a means of social control, is an instrument of unequal justice for people of color, perpetuating the differentiation and discrimination that has long permeated much of American life. The historical approach is skillfully used to illustrate how racial prejudice and inequality continues to reinvent itself through *institutional racism,* the result of a long history of overt racism that now persists through laws, policies, practices and procedures that continue to produce unequal results. Mann's well-written work on the subject not only explains the consequences of this phenomenon in the creation of the conditions for the flowering of disproportionate minority involvement in crime, but is also a call to action for all those who care about social justice. Mann defined *institutional racism* as follows:

> Inherent in *racism* is an assumption that race determines one's traits and abilities, and that a particular race is inherently superior to another race on the basis of those characteristics. More importantly, the group that defines itself as superior controls all institutional power. *Institutional racism* is present when the social, political, economic, religious, and educational structures, or the major institutions in a society benefit a particular race-the "white" race in the United States-at the expense of other races (Mann 1995c: 260).

In keeping with her distinctive holistic approach, Mann's most comprehensive statement in this area, her book entitled *Unequal Justice, A Question of Color* (1993), provides a comparative analysis of the criminal justice processing of all racial and ethnic minorities (including subgroups of immigrants) for which data is available. Her book is divided into two parts (with three chapters each) entitled: "Minorities and Crime" and "The Response to Minority Crime" which are closely interwoven. Mann defines and discusses the meaning and significance of race and uses the historical approach to reveal the persistence of oppression, differentiation, discrimination, and exclusion in the experiences of minority groups with American culture and institutions.

A distinctive feature of Mann's work is that she broadens traditional specifications of minority groups to include not only African-Americans, Native-Americans, Asian-Americans, and Hispanic- Americans but also a variety of identifiable sub-groups within these larger groups who are present in the U.S. population (Mann 1993). She then analyzes official statistics and reviews the existing studies to reveal not only the entrenchment of institutionalized racism at every stage of the criminal justice process, but biases in the way minority crime is measured, analyzed, and explained by researchers and the resulting impact of race-based interpretations on policy making and the administration of justice. After demonstrating the role of the state in the production of minority crime, Mann ends by conducting a scathing review of current corrections, policies and practices.

The inclusion of a minority perspective at the end of each of the six chapters in this book provides a distinctive African-American definition of the minority experience, one that has traditionally been excluded from the vast majority of criminal justice literature.

In a separate article entitled "A Minority View of Juvenile Justice" (1994), apparently in response to anti-crime legislation mandating more punitive treatment for juveniles in Indiana, Mann addressed the problems faced by African-American youths in the juvenile justice system. African- American youths, like their adult counterparts, are over-represented at all stages of the criminal justice process. According to recent estimates, minority youth account for about half of all juveniles held in public facilities (Beck et al. 1988). After discussing the dismal state of affairs for these youths, Mann provided an example of the apathy and hypocrisy that characterizes state responses to federal criminal justice initiatives, when she detailed the failure of the majority of states to avail themselves of funding opportunities offered by the Office of Juvenile Justice and Delinquency Prevention. These funds had been earmarked for the implementation of policies, procedures, and practices to reduce minority involvement in the juvenile justice system, but many states did not comply with the requirements in order to avail themselves of the funding. This incongruence between policy and practice creates confusion as to whether the reduction of the disproportionate involvement of minority youth in crime has been abandoned as a worthwhile objective, and instead, incapacitation through warehousing has been chosen as a more beneficial enterprise (Mann 1993).

Mann has devoted considerable effort to unraveling the often complex mechanisms that produce unequal justice on the basis of color in the United States. The constantly recurring "waves" of discrimination research (MacLean et al. 1990b:2) spanning several decades attests to the recognition of the pervasive impact of race relations on every aspect of life in America. In discussing the current race relations crisis in the field of criminal justice, Walker (1996:1) cites the celebrated African-American scholar W.E.B. Du Bois as designating "the color line" to be the leading problem of the twentieth century. Mann has made a lasting contribution to the definition and explanation of the significance of "the color line" in the dispensation of criminal justice.

## CONCLUSION

The need for African-American perspectives of crime and justice in America is clearly demonstrated not only by the inequities suffered by this group, who are the most populous in the nation's "warehouses," but also by the dismal failure of existing policies and practices that are almost wholly defined by Eurocentric perspectives. The writings of Coramae Richey Mann, presented herein, illustrate the uniqueness of the African-American definition of the situation and the need to adopt a broader explanation of crime and criminal justice in America that would include structural inequality, economic disadvantage, racial and ethnic differentiation, and differential treatment at all stages of the criminal justice process.

Mann has covered every aspect of the criminal justice system in her work, focusing in particular on the criminality of women and minorities, and their experiences in the criminal justice system. Although she has devoted a great deal of time to the very worthwhile task of filling the gaps in the literature with reference to minority crime, Mann has always maintained the need for a holistic and inclusive approach. She has made substantial contributions towards the dismantling of the mythology that pervades the literature concerning the experience of minorities in the criminal justice system, but only in the interest of truth and accuracy, and for the furtherance of understanding and justice. Mann is essentially a humanist and her work is an important addition to an emerging and distinctive minority perspective on crime and justice in America.

## NOTES

1     Mann adopts the definition *of victim precipitation* proposed by Wolfgang (1958) whereby the victim causes his own demise by commencing the violent assault that ends in death.

2     Also called "battered wife syndrome" or "battered person syndrome," this defense is used to justify criminal homicide after allegedly long periods of physical abuse. Mann did not investigate this explanation for homicide in the cases she studied, but she discussed its seeming inapplicability to the facts of those cases.

3     Illegal drugs include heroin, methadone, amphetamines, methaqualone, barbiturates, cocaine, PCP, LSDF and marijuana/hashish.

4     "Murder" includes (1) intentionally causing the death of another person without extreme provocation or legal justification, (2) causing the death of another while committing or attempting to commit another crime, and (3) non negligent or voluntary manslaughter. Charges stated in order of seriousness are first-degree murder (the most serious), second-degree or other murder and voluntary or non negligent manslaughter (the least serious).

5     The "subculture of violence" theory was developed by Marvin Wolfgang and Franco Ferracuti (1967) and proposes that the existence of a subculture of violence can be determined by examination of the social groups and individuals who manifest the highest rates of criminal violence--homicide. Members of the subculture hold values which encourage physical aggression and favor the resort to lethal violence without the concomitant feelings of guilt, shame and anxiety experienced by members of the dominant culture. The theory has been applied to Blacks and Hispanics and is still influential among contemporary explanations of the determinants of violence.

6     Mortality statistics are compiled by the Centers for Disease Control's
      National Center for Health Statistics from information collected on all
      death certificates and filed in the 50 states and the District of Columbia in
      accordance with World Health Organization regulations.

# REFERENCES

Adler, Freda. 1975. *Sisters in Crime: The Rise of the New Female Criminal.* New York: McGraw-Hill.

Beck, Allen, Susan Kline and Lawrence Greenfleld. 1988. *Survey of Youth in Custody, 1987.* Washington D.C.: Bureau of Justice Statistics.

Binder, Arnold. 1988. *Juvenile Delinquency: Historical, Cultural, Legal Perspectives.* New York: Macmillan.

Chambliss, William J., and Robert B. Seidman. 1971. *Law, Order and Power.* Reading, Mass.: Addison-Wesley.

Cowie, John, Valerie Cowie and Elliot Slater. 1968. *Delinquency in Girls.* London: Heinemann.

Dawson, John M. and Barbara Boland. 1993. *Murder in Large Urban Counties, 1988.* Washington, D.C.: Bureau of Justice Statistics.

Dawson, John M. and Patrick A. Langan. 1994. *Murder in Families.* Washington, D.C.: Bureau of Justice Statistics.

Federal Bureau of Investigation. 1971. *Crime in the United States, 1970: Uniform Crime Reports.* Washington, D.C.: U.S. Government Printing Office.

Federal Bureau of Investigation. 1986. *Crime in the United States, 1985: Uniform Crime Reports.* Washington, D.C.: U.S. Government Printing Office.

Federal Bureau of Investigation. 1994. *Crime in the United States, 1993: Uniform Crime Reports.* Washington, D.C.: U.S. Government Printing Office.

Federal Bureau of Investigation. 1995. *Crime in the United States, 1994: Uniform Crime Reports.* Washington, D.C.: U.S. Government Printing Office.

Fingerhut, Lois A. 1993. "The Impact of Homicide on Life Changes: International, Intranational and Demographic Comparisons." In Carolyn Rebecca Block and Richard Block, eds., *Questions and Answers in Lethal and Non-Lethal Violence.* Washington, D.C.; National Institute of Justice, U.S. Department of Justice.

French, Laurence. 1977. "An Assessment of the Black Female Prisoner in the South." *Journal of Women in Culture and Society.* Vol.3, No.21: 483-488.

_____. 1978. "The Incarcerated Black Female: The Case of Social Double Jeopardy." *Journal of Black Studies* 8 (3): 321-335.

Greenfleld, Lawrence A. and Stephanie Minor-Harper. 1991. *Women in Prison.* Washington, D.C.: Bureau of Justice Statistics.

Hill, Gary D. and Elizabeth Crawford. 1990. "Women, Race and Crime. *Criminology* 28 (4): 601-25.

Laub, John H. and Joan McDermott. 1985. "An Analysis of Serious Crime by Young Black Women." *Criminology* 23(1): 81-98.

Lombroso, Caesar and Ferrero, William. 1920. *The Female Offender.* New York: Appleton.

MacLean, Brian and Dragan Milovanovic, eds. 1990a. *Racism, Empiricism and Criminal Justice.* Vancouver: The Collective Press.

_____. 1990b. "The Anatomy of the 'No Discrimination Thesis.'" In Brian MacLean and Dragan Milovanovic, eds., *Racism, Empiricism and Criminal Justice.* Vancouver: The Collective Press.

Mann, Coramae R. 1976. *The Juvenile Female in The Judicial Process.* Ph.D. Dissertation. University of Illinois at Chicago Circle.

_____. 1989. "Minority and Female: A Criminal Justice Double Bind." *Social Justice 16: 95-114.*

_____. 1990a. "Black Female Homicide in the United States." *Journal of Interpersonal Violence 5* (2): 176-201.

_____. 1990b. "Random Thoughts on the Ongoing Wilbanks-Mann Discourse." In Brian MacLean and Dragan Milovanovic, eds., *Racism, Empiricism and Criminal Justice.* Vancouver: The Collective Press.

_____. 1993. *Unequal Justice: A Question of* Color. Bloomington: Indiana University Press.

_____. 1994. "A Minority View of Juvenile 'Justice.'" *Washington and Lee*

*Law Review 51:* 465-478.

_____. 1995a. "Women of Color and the Criminal Justice System." In Barbara Raffel price and Natalie J. Sokoloft, eds., *The Criminal Justice System and Women.* New York: McGraw-Hill, Inc.

_____. 1995b. "Seventeen White Men and Me." In Ann Goetting and Sarah Fenstermaker, eds., *Individual Voices; Collective Visions:* Fifty *Years of Women in Sociology.* Philadelphia: Temple University Press.

Mann, Coramae R. 1995c. "The Contribution of Institutionalized Racism to Minority Crime." In Darnell F. Hawkins, ed., *Ethnicity Race and Crime, Perspectives Across Time and Place.* New York: State University of New York Press.

_____. 1996. *When Women Kill.* New York: State University of New York Press.

McClain Paula D. 1982. "Black Females and Lethal Violence: Has Time Changed the Circumstances Under Which They Kill?" *Omega* 13 (1): *13-25.*

Noblit, George W. and Janie M. Burcart. 1976. "Women and Crime: 1960-1970." *Social Science Quarterly* 56: 650-657.

Pollak, Otto. *1950. The Criminality of Women.* Philadelphia: University of Pennsylvania Press.

Pollak, Otto. ed. 1969. *Family Dynamics and Female Sexual Delinquency.* Palo Alto, California: Science and Behavior Books.

Quinney, Richard. 1970. *The Social Reality of Crime.* Boston: Little Brown & Co.

Riege, Mary. 1972. "Parental Affection and Juvenile Delinquency in Girls." *British Journal of Criminology* 12: 55-73.

Schmalleger, Frank. 1977. *Criminal Justice Today.* New Jersey: Prentice Hall.

Senna, Joseph J. and Larry J. Siegel. 1996. *Introduction to Criminal Justice.* St. Paul, *MN* West Publishing Co.

Simon, Rita James. 1975. *The Contemporary Woman and Crime.* Washington D.C.: U.S. Government Printing Office.

_____. 1976. "Women and Crime Revisited." *Social Science Quarterly* 56: 658-63.

Smart, Carol. 1979. "The New Female Criminal: Reality or Myth." *British Journal of Criminology 19:50-59.*

Snyder, Howard N., and Melissa Sickmund. 1995. *Juvenile Offenders and Victims: A National Report* Washington, D.C.: National Center for Juvenile Justice.

Steffensmeier, Darrell J. 1980a. "Assessing the Impact of the Women's Movement on Sex-Based Differences in the Handling of Adult Criminal Defendants." *Crime and Delinquency* 26: 344-57.

_____. 1980b. "Sex-Based differences in patterns of Adult Crime, 1965-77: A Review and Assessment." *Social forces* 58: 1080-1108.

Steffensmeier, Darrell J. 1981. "Crime and the Contemporary Woman: An Analysis of Changing Levels of Female Property Crime, 1960-1975." In *Women and Crime in America.* New York: Macmillan.

Thomas, William I. 1907. *Sex and Society.* Boston: Little, Brown & Co.

_____. 1923. *The Unadjusted Girl* New York: Harper & Row.

Walker, Samuel, Cassia Spohn and Miriam DeLone. 1996. *The Color of Justice: Race, Ethnicity and Crime in America.* Belmont, CA: Wadsworth Publishing Co.

Wilbanks, William. 1987. *The Myth of a Racist Criminal Justice System.* Monterey: Brooks/Cole.

Wolfgang, Marvin E. 1958. *Patterns in Criminal Homicide.* Montclair, NJ: Patterson Smith.

# CHAPTER EIGHT

## Nwapa and Gender, Culture, and Modernization:
## A Case Study of *Efuru* and *Idu*
### Kofi Johnson
### Babatunde Oyinade

There has been a curious indifference to female voices in the literary circle in Africa. The first female writer in Nigeria to break the mold is Flora Nwapa. Her works are the most ambitious attempt to provide readers with the nature of patriarchy and gender among the Igbo people in colonial Nigeria.

In this chapter, we will examine two of Flora Nwapa's works: *Efuru* and *Idu*. Each of these works is a novel of development and discusses the harsh social reality that pervades the people of Oguta in the former Eastern Nigeria. The chapter concludes with a brief discussion of the significance of the female writers in contemporary African literary tradition. In addition, the chapter analyses the sociosexual themes which dominate oral theme of Nwapa and the impact of patriarchy on gender in Uguta.

Flora Nwapa was born in the former Eastern Nigeria in 1913. She received her basic education at the Methodist Girl's High School, Lagos. Enrolled at University of Ibadan where she studied literature. In 1953, she attended Edinburg University in Britain where she obtained a diploma in education. Thereafter, she engaged in various occupations such as teaching, publishing, and working with the Nigerian government. At the end of the civil war in Nigeria, she was appointed a minister in the East Central State government. Nwapa wrote several novels but she is well known in writers' circles for *Efuru* and *Idu* which were published in 1966 and 1970 respectively.

## BACKGROUND

Before we proceed to examine Nwapa's two major works, it is instructive to pose the following question: Is suppression of women in Igboland a legacy of the colonial administration or the legacy of patriarchal society as exemplified by the traditional custom's of the Igbo? The answer to this question would enhance our understanding of the status of women in the Igbo community and Africa as a whole. As Van Allen points out in her article: "the British colonialists introduced sexist Victorian values into all aspects of the life (religious, economic, and political) of the colonized Igbo." In support of this viewpoint, Okonjo noted that "such Victorian values extolled the ideology that 'women's place is in the home'." (See Lebeuf, 1960:96 and also Okonjo, 1976:46)

If we want to understand the history of a people as Karl Marx puts it, one must understand their modes of production. It is their mode of production that defines the class that one belongs. One of the premise of the argument that is presented here is that the policies and practices of the colonialists fundamentally reshaped gender relations in traditional societies (cited in Tetreault, 1994:65). This argument has been advanced by writers such as Flora Nwapa and Ama Ata Aidoo (cited in Frank, 1987: 15). This did not mean that prior to colonial rule, Africans lived in an ideal state. In Igbo society for example, there was a strict gender-based division of labor in which "women owned their surplus crops and their market profits, while men controlled the more valuable yams and palm product (Van Allen, 1976:77). The surpluses could not be transformed into capital investments. Rather, they ploughed them back to the community through fees, rituals, and wedding ceremonies (Ibid.).

This gender-based division of labor recognized women as a critical component of the economy in the political economy. For this reason, Igbo women held certain positions in the community such as: participating in discussions of public policy, representing women in the council of elders, and they possessed the freedom of defending and protecting their own economic rights (see Robertson et al, 1986: 239). Van Allen captured the positions of Igbo women in pre-colonial days in these words:

> Women as well as men thus has access to political participation; for women as well as for men, public status was to a great extent achieved, not ascribed. A woman's status was determined more by her own achievements than by those of her husband'. ( Van Allen, 1976:67).

In other words, Igbo society was "dual sex institution" as Okonjo observed.

As the colonial government gained foot-hold in the Igboland where leadership was informal and the system condoned equal balance of power between male and female, the British introduced a system of indirect rule to enable them to govern the people effectively and for administrative purposes. Since there were no identified emirs or obas in the former Eastern Nigeria, most of the Igboland was ruled by warrant chiefs. This system also came with the introduction of native administration. Consequently, Igboland was divided into Native Court Areas which lumped together many unrelated villages, thereby violated the autonomy of the villages. This set the stage for subjugation of women by men in Igboland. It should also be pointed out that the concept of warrant chiefs to oversee the people was fragrant violation of Igbo tradition, because for one man to maintain order was an aberration in the traditional sense. The warrant officers were seen as a front for the colonial conquerors.

Women suffered the most in the hands of the warrant chiefs. They were forced against their will not to make choice as to whom to marry. That is to say, judgments were given in favor of the men that they had rejected their hands in marriage. An attempt by the British to impose tax without representation in Igboland led to the famous Aba Riot in 1929, that was planned and choreographed by Aba women. It spread more than 600 miles radius before it was brought under control. More than 60 women were killed (see Okonjo,1976). When the authorities embarked upon investigating the source of the riot, men fearing that those who had organized the riot would be punished refused to offer any information. As a result, the majority of the British Officers thought men had organized the riot, and that women were merely used by men as surrogates. When reform came in 1933, women were ignored in their political role. The reform implemented by the colonialists favored men and women became the sacrificial lambs. This created a system that turned women in to second class citizens.

By refusing women to actively participate in the political processes, and by not appointing them to any important posts, and neglecting their education and employment, the British in Igboland pursued a policy of alienation and exclusion of Igbo women from the economic and political arenas. Thus, began a system of sex and class stratification in Igboland. Women could no longer compete with men in public decision making, because they lack requisite resources such as education, economic power and employment. According to Van Allen, 1976, "this economic imbalance in resources was increased by other facets of British colonialism-economic 'penetration' and missionary influence" (Van Allen, 1976:75). The exclusion of women from education reflected both sexism and class bias of British society.

There is an abundance of evidence that African women participated in politics. In the Niger and Chad regions and in Hausaland, history is abound with women who founded cities, led migration and conquered kingdoms. In Kastina now a part of Nigeria, Queen Amina became famous in the 15th century through the conquest of other Hausa states (Sweetman,1984:25). In Zimbabwe, the first woman to organize resistance against white settlers in the former Southern Rhodesia was Nehanda. It can be argued that many girls and women who took part in the liberation of Zimbabwe in the 1970s, drew their inspiration from Nehanda. In the former Gold Coast, now Ghana, Yaa Asantewa of Asante led her people in a fierce battle to keep the British abay from gaining foothold in the Gold Coast. This bird's eye survey of African women in pre-colonial days should provide us with sufficient examples that women played important roles in various pre-colonial African communities. It also shows that "there are no valid historical grounds for explaining the present lack of interest in political matters so often found among African women as heritage of the past" (cited in Pauline,1963:96). Added to this, the colonial power imposed partriarchical customs and laws that bred women oppression in Igboland and the colonial period created economies dependent on export crops and raw material that caused class stratification and gender-bias against women in African society.

The background analysis presented here can be suggested as the basis for Nwapa's new literary paradigm which was intended to explain the unknown facts which were neglected by contemporary male African writers. Significantly, Nwapa uses *Efuru* and *Idu* to reconstruct historical episode that had been tampered or distorted by male writers and to write history from a female point of view.

## *EFURU*

*Efuru* is the first completed novel written by a Nigerian woman. This makes Nwapa the first Nigerian female novelist in modern times. It is interesting to ask why it took Nigerian women a long time to appear on the literary scene, almost ten years after the appearance of Achebe's *Things Fall Apart*? There are many explanations to this question. The plausible factors include the male-biased nature of the educational system. This was fueled by the colonial policy that favored men's education over women. Consequently, this cut women off from the writing world. The same male bias extended to the post-independent Nigeria (cited in Stratton, 1994). This was clearly illustrated by Ayesha Imam's speech at the Third Annual Conference of Women held in Nigeria in 1984. Imam refers to the notion of equality of opportunity in education as a "myth." She said that "Not only are there more boys than girls in schools, but also there are more schools (and school places) for boys" (cited in Stratton, 1994:80). She added that 76 percent of families "would educate their sons but not their daughters, if finances were limited." Stratton, 1994, added to this, is the social prejudice that limits women's access to education. Another factor is the critical devaluation of women's writing on the literary circle. This was evident in the reviews of Efuru by male reviewers like Eldred Jones and Eustace Palmer. Both reviewers rebuked Nwapa for focusing on the "women's world." This critical assault damaged Nwapa's reputation as a writer. For example, Palmer says that "the bulk of (*Efuru*) is unnecessary" (Stratton, 1994).

*Efuru* is Nwapa's first novel. It breaks new thematic and stylistic ground by focusing on women's longing for children to make their lives whole and personal emancipation. Nwapa explores traditional rules, modes, and codes of the Igbo communities. Her choice of subject shocked many reviewers who condemned her work because it deals with gender. As a result, Nwapa was not well received on the literary circle, until recently when her subject matters gained currency among feminist writers. Reviewers and scholars then began to treat her as a serious writer.

*Efuru* portrays several aspects of life in Igboland. It deals with the tradition and corporate life of the people of Uguta where the novel gets its setting. The heroine is put in various situations in which she interacts with large numbers of people in her community. The novel proper begins with the heroine meeting Adizua, a poor farmer, and few days later, she marries without parental consent. The next Nkwo day, that is market day, Efuru moves to her husband's house. With this background, the gossips of her defiance and breaking of the tradition begin to billow in the air in Oguta of Efuru.

As the novel develops, Efuru becomes the dominant personality while Adizua plays the role of a docile husband. Efuru dictates the pace and the directions she wants her life to take. Adizua, a farmer by occupation, wants to be a prosperous farmer but his wife would not live on the farm with him because she believes that farm work is not cut out for her. When Efuru finds life in the village boring Adizua moves to town, where Efuru can pursue her trade. Having violated the traditional rule, Efuru refuses to play the traditional role assigned to women of Oguta. Efuru's inability to have a child created some difficulties for the couple and the community as a whole. Adizua downplayed the barrenness of his wife at the beginning. Efuru consults debia-a traditional medicine man who assures her that she would have a child. Meanwhile, Efuru becomes pregnant and she gives birth to Ogonim. Notwithstanding the arrival of Ogonim, Adizua deserts his wife to assert his manhood, or to escape living under the shadow of his wife. The desertion of Adizua is very devastating for Efuru. She decides to conduct a background investigation about Adizua. What she should have done in the beginning before marrying Adizua as tradition dictates in Uguta. She discovers from her mother-in-law that Adizua has followed the foot steps of his father (Taiwo, 1984). Efuru leaves her marital home and returns to her father. The marriage also runs into problem after the birth of Ogonim. It becomes clear that Efuru has difficulty in having another child. Although she made more money, she discovers that money cannot buy her happiness.

> What is money? Can a bag of money go for an errand for you. Can a bag of money look after you in your old age? Can a bag of money mourn you when you are dead? A child is more valuable than money (Nwapa: 1966).

Faced with her first marriage ending in fiasco. Efuru begins to accept the reality of life. She becomes sober and softens her aggressiveness. She now accepts polygamy as a way of life. She says: "It is only a bad woman who wants her husband to herself" (Nwapa, 1966). Her botched marriage taught her lessons on how to handle her second marriage. She marries Eneberi. Eneberi is a semi-literate man who went to a mission school and changed his name to Gilbert. He is a Christian who displays his love openly to the annoyance of the Uguta people that he and his wife become objects of gossips by the villagers.

> "I like them, one woman said of Gilbert and Efuru were leaving the stream."
>
> "When two people live like that, then the world is worth living in," another added.
>
> "What do you admire in the lives of those two?" Omirima asked contemptuously.
>
> "Do you know what they went through last night? Don't be carried away by the fact that they come to the stream together and swim and play in the deep."
>
> "You are right," one of the women said.
>
> "Have they children?" another asked.
>
> "Children? You don't pluck children from a tree you know. You don't fight for them either. Money cannot buy them. Happiness cannot give you children. Children indeed, they have no children."
>
> "What is he doing? Foolish man. He sits down there and refuses to do anything. He doesn't see young girls all over the place to take one as wife. It is their business not mine" (Ibid., 174-175).

This dialogue illustrates the kind of gossips that permeate the community. The villagers are self-contained, and ignorant about outsiders. They are happy within their community. Their forte is strong family attachment. They revere and worship the spirit of their ancestors. In time of adversities, they consult with the medicine man called debia who assures them as to what rituals should be performed to ward off the adversities. Significantly, the community is heirachical in structure. In such a rural setting, gossips become a way of life to know what goes on in their community.

There is no question that Efuru and Eneberi are in love but they have different orientations which set the stage to ruin their relationship (Taiwo: 1984). Childlessness becomes the theme and problematic in their marriage. Meanwhile, Eneberi has child with another woman outside the marriage, a fact that was unknown to Efuru. The differences that exist between Eneberi and his wife place a wedge in their marriage. For example, Eneberi is a modern man, with a western education. On the other hand, Efuru is a traditionalist who does not possess a western education. So when Eneberi accused Efuru of adultery her pride was hurt. She packs her belongings and heads to her father's house. With two failed marriages, Efuru devotes her life to serve the goddess of the lake: Uhamiri.

The actors in the novel are mainly women. Apart from Efuru there are other actors who play important roles.  For example, Ajanapu is depicted as independent, a counselor, and a woman who knows about Uguta. She is projected as giving support to Efuru in time of difficulties. Women in Efurus Uguta are very industrious. Consider this: "Women in our town are very industrious. They rise when the cock crows" (Nwapa, 1966).

Efuru is a street-wise woman of Uguta. Her mother died when she was young. She was raised by her father and learned everything from those she interacted with in her adolescent years.

## *IDU*

Idu is similar to Efuru. The main characters in *Idu* are Adiewere and Idu. They are presented as a newly married couple who are experiencing the joy of marriage. Adiewere, we are told, is a good man. There is no such man like him. Idu is being described as beautiful. The couple is very happy with each other. Their happiness begins to chip away when Idu is assumed to be barren. Just as childlessness plays an important role in *Efuru*, it also plays an important role in *Idu*. The Igbo custom does not accept happiness in marriage unless it is blessed with children. Societal expectation that the couple must have a child puts an avalanche of wedge in their marriage. Adiewere is not a polygamist but because of societal expectation, he is forced to take another wife. Idu even encourages him to take another wife in order to satisfy his people. This forces Adiewere to embark on a drinking spree as a way of escaping from reality. This is followed by late night outings and parties with his age-group. Finally he contracted a mysterious disease which leads to his sudden death. The death of Adiewere causes Idu to become demented. Life without Adiewere becomes unbearable to Idu. At Adiewere's death Idu has this to say:

> I will not weep. That is not what we agreed-
> Adiewere and I planned things together. We did not
> plan this. We did not plan that he would leave me
> today and go the land of the dead. Who will I live
> with? Who will be my husband, the father of my
> only son? Who will talk to me at night? What are
> you telling me? Asking me to weep? To weep for
> my husband? I was with him only yesterday. We
> did not sleep early. We talked making plans and
> today he is dead, he is a corpse lying there, a corpse,
> and you tell me to weep for him (Nwapa, 1970).

Idu died a few days after she made that moving speech expressing how Adiewere's death destroyed her power to continue to live.

The novelist presents us with Amarajeme and Ojiugbo. They are a married couple. During their marriage, Ojiugbo fails to bear Amarajeme a child after several years of marriage. Ojiugbo elopes with another man. Ojiugbo refuses to believe that his wife was gone forever. When it becomes clear that his wife will not return and of the news that his wife has a child for another man, he becomes despondent. Amarajeme hangs himself because Ojiugbo has not kept the secret of his impotence.

In *Idu*, Nwapa tells us about the solidarity of the villagers when Ijeoma, Idu's son is missing. The entire community becomes involved in the search for Ijeoma. This is presented by the novelist to portray the solidarity that exists before the arrival of the colonialists. According to Taiwo (1984), "The genuiness of the people's distress and the thorough energetic manner in which they show their concern attest to their love and respect for Idu."

## DISCUSSION

The late fifties and the sixties saw the first crops of African novelists. Most of the novelists were influenced by the experiences of events in their communities. Leading the way was Chinua Achebe. In Achebe's *Things Fall Apart*, he discussed a missionary venture designed to prepare the natives to face the future in positive frame of mind, with pride and belief in themselves. The writings of these novelists are characterized by the use of very simple language which reflects traditional speech patterns of Africans. At first, the works become boring and insipid to the foreigners particularly the use of proverbs-Achebe refers to them as "the palm-oil  with which words are eaten" (Owomoyela, 1979:79). The Yorubas characterize proverbs as the horses of speech through which lost words are being retrieved (Owomoyela, 1979). All in all, the use of proverbs and simplicity of the language are an attempt to capture the romance and elegance of traditional communications. The early African novelists were mostly men who tended to pay attention in their writings on social, historical, and political rather than on domestic themes or women. The trail blazer on women issues is Nwapa.

In *Efuru* and *Edu*, Nwapa presents us with writings outside the narrative domain of male writers. Her protagonists are assigned befitting roles dealing with decision making and jurors of their society. In both novels, she discusses every day life of women within their compounds. Both unfold as conversations. Unlike her counterparts who treat women as objects to be desired, taken as wives against their wills, captured as booty of wars, and are heard only when spoken to, as exemplified by Achebe's *Things Fall Apart* or *Jagua Nana* by Cyprain Ekwensi whose work depicts a middle-aged prostitute, Nwapa focuses on the important roles played by women. She portrays them as active and not passive objects in the pre-colonial communities. Like Achebe's work, however, both *Efuru* and *Idu* are set in rural Igboland which Nwapa calls Uguta. By contrast, Nwapa focuses on women. She breaks new ground by turning conflict and disillusionment of women in a male dominated culture by emphasizing the female point of view to the issues of cultural conflict and economic change. It should be pointed out that Nwapa's interest goes beyond women subjects. "What distinguishes her from others in the 'Igbo school' are the ways in which she has used the choric language to enable and to empower her presentation, creating the effect of a woman's presence within her text, while bringing home her subject matter by evoking the vocality of women's everyday existence" (Nasta,1992:12). The women of Nwapa "occupy a self-enclosed, stable domestic domain-custom and environment are known to all speakers and few characters are unfamiliar" (Nasta, 1992). The women in Nwapa's novels are also concerned with childbearing, being good mothers and wives. This is illustrated in these words by Efuru:

> But thank God my womb carried a baby for nine
> months. Thank God I had this baby and she was a
> normal baby. It would have been dreadful if I had
> been denied the joy of motherhood. And now when
> mothers talk about their experience in childbirth, I
> can share their happiness with them, though
> Ogonim is no more (Nwapa, 1966:207).

Apart from motherhood and childbearing, *Efuru* and *Idu* are novels of defiance and development. That is, the women seek independence and self-actualization than playing the roles assigned by their community. *Efuru* begins with the heroine marrying without parental consent. When her husband left her she defies Igbo custom by leaving her marital home to her father, unafraid of the gossips. When her second husband accused her of adultery she divorced her. Idu is also a novel defiant of societal beliefs. When Idu's husband died, "she resolves that the relationship provided by the marriage was more important to her than bearing children" (Nasta, 1992:18). Efuru is abound with criticisms of custom and authority. For example:

> Why the government does not allow us to drink our
> home-made gin. I do not know. The Government is
> strange. Doesn't know that it cannot stop us from
> cooking gin; that our people will continue to go to

jail instead of giving up completely. If they must
stop us from cooking gin, then the white man's gin
and his schnapps should be sold cheap (Nwapa,
1966:150).

As the colonial government gained foothold in Igboland things began to
change for the people of Uguta. The natives began to embrace Christianity and
this resulted in those evils common with western culture. Efuru describes those
changes with the arrival of Christianity and its impact on Oguta people, and how
it tends to destroy the traditional beliefs in these words:

If your property was stolen you simply went to one
of the idol, and prayed him to visit the thief. Before
two or three days, you recovered your property. But
these church goers have spoilt everything. They tell
us our gods have no powers, so our people continue
to steal (Nwapa, 1966:223)

Efuru's observation illustrates the cultural conflict and disillusionment by
the Igbo people with the clash of two civilizations, the European and African
cultures.

The argument that western education debases traditional culture has
generated endless debate among many writers. Some even go further to argue that
the entrenched partriachal culture came with the white colonialists. Nwapa holds
that it came from the colonialists. This is illustrated when two women engage in
small talk about Amede daughter-in-law's behavior:

She went to school and so she thinks she knows
everything. She is lazy. Have you ever known a
woman, brought up in our town who sleeps until the
sun is up?"
"No, impossible. Who sleeps until the sun is
up?" Amede asked unbelievingly.
"My daugter-in-law, Amede, my daughter-
in-law. I have talked and talked, my son does not
want to listen to me. Please help me to talk. Go
there now, and you will be told by one of the
numerous servants that she in bed sleeping."

"This is bad. She is unlike our women. Where did
she learn this foreign bad behaviour? I thank God
my daughter-in-law does not sleep till sunrise."

"She learnt it from the white woman. That is
what I told her. I said to her, you are not an idle
white woman. Women of our town are very
industrious. They rise when the cock crows.
Husbands of white women are rich, so their wives
can afford to be lazy. An idle woman is dangerous,
so I told to her face."

Yes, an idle woman is dangerous. I pity these
white women you know. How can one sit down in a
big house all oneself and do nothing? It must be
difficult life," Amede said (Nwapa, 1970:245).

Nwapa shows in the above conversation that western education is the
source of domestication of women that imprisons them to gender assigned role.
Significantly, it condemns women to confinement in houses owned by men where
they sit by themselves doing nothing. In addition, Nwapa perceives western
behavior as dangerous to the emancipation of women because it breeds laziness
and idleness. She writes that "Women in our town are very industrious" (Nwapa,
1966). This is to demonstrate that Uguta women draw their source of strength and
self-worth from hardwork rather than depending on men for their livelihood.

At the center of Efuru's story is Uhamiri-a water deity. Nwapa presents
this deity as a figure not to be desired by male but as a symbol of freedom and
independence of women (Stratton: 92). The water deity is also mentioned in *Idu*.
Another aspect that plays an important role in *Efuru* is the absence of a mother to
guide Efuru in the world of fathers. Perhaps, this can be attributed to her
rebellious attitude against her community. The first act of rebellion occurs when
she marries Adizua, a poor farmer, without her father's permission. It becomes an
insult to her family when Adizua does not pay bride price. The second act of
rebellion takes place when Efuru becomes pregnant. Upon constant advice from
her husband to quit working, Efuru insists on continuing her trade until the arrival
of Ogonim. The third act of rebellion occurs when Ogonim is born. She

immediately returns to trading and chooses someone to look after her daughter. Nwapa's rationale in bringing out these rebellious acts is to establish the independence of Uguta women and their defiance of gender assigned roles. They also illustrate that Uguta women had already shattered the "ceiling glass" of gender role when feminism was still at its infancy in the West. It can also be interpreted that the acts marked development in the lives of Nwapa's women. It should be pointed out that whenever tradition stifles their individuality, Nwapa's protagonists step out of them to adopt alternative means that best enable them to express their personalities. A case in point is illustrated when Adizua deserts Efuru. She continues to live in his house. She even goes in search for her. After waiting for two years to avoid being accused of impropriety by her community, she returns to her father's house, an indication that she is ready to take other prospective suitors (Davies et al: 1986).

The troubling aspect of *Efuru* and *Idu* is that men protagonists are painted as imbecile, poor and unfit . It can be argued that this was the reason that Nwapa received poor evaluations from male reviewers. This is perhaps the weakness of Nwapa's Uguta in her stories. Credits are not given to men. But even then, unlike Buchi Emecheta, Nwapa presents women in a more realistic African centered manner.

## CONCLUSION

In this chapter, we have made attempts to emphasize that history does not support that African women were not political animals, and that the colonial masters imposed partriarchical customs and laws that made them to be passive in the present day political processes. Significantly, Nwapa's *Efuru* and *Idu* are novels of development. She is the first African woman to have her novel published in Britain in the post-independent Nigeria when literary activities were dominated by male writers.

The word development as used in this chapter connotes redefinition of women's roles in a patriarchal society. It is not used here as a transference to a technological base. They are novels of development because the main protagonists exhibit norms contrary to the traditional assigned chores. The main protagonists defy what their culture stands for and the women towed independent paths.

It can be stated that the primary aim of Nwapa in the two novels is to challenge the dominance of male in the new Nigeria. In addition, it can be argued that Nwapa has written the novels particularly Efuru to refute idealization of motherhood and to rebuke men writers such as Achebe for their shortcomings for not portraying women protagonists in befitting manners, because male authors tend to fall into depicting women as lovers, wives, and appendages of men. Nwapa changed these assigned traditional roles in these two novels. The works are attempts to tell her counterparts that women also played significant roles in the struggle for independence and that their voices should not be side-tracked by male writers. Nwapa's treatment of gender gives other women a paradigm in which to construct their works. As a result of her pioneer works, an army of women writers have emerged in Africa. A cursory role call of such women would include Buchi Emecheta, Ama Ataa Aidoo, Ifeoma Okoye, Zulu Sofola, just to name a few who have become recognized because of the thematic styles that Nwapa pioneered. She showed the light so that other African women writers can follow. Since the appearance of her first novel, there have emerged an avalanche of women writers trumpeting the thematic styles of Nwapa ,thereby mapping out a new era for African women on the literary scene.

## REFERENCES

Davies, Carole Boyce. 1986. *Npambika: Studies of Women in African Literature* Trenton, N.J.: Africa World Press, Inc.

Frank, Katherine. 1987. "Women Without Men: The Feminist Novel in Africa" in Jones, Eldred. Durosimi, *Women in African Literature Today*. London, England: James Currey Ltd. African World Press.

Lebeuf, Annie. M.D. 1960. "The Role of Women in the Political Organization of African Cities," cited in Pauline, Denise. *Women of Tropical Africa*. Beckley, Cal.: University of California.

Okonjo, Kamene. 1976. "The Dual-Sex Political System in Operation: Igbo Women and Community Politics in Western Niger," cited in, Hafkin, Nancy. J., Bay, Edna. J. *Women in Africa: Studies in Social and Economic Change*. Stanford, Cal:Standford University Press.

Nasta, Susheila. ed., 1991. *Motherlands: Black Women's Writing from Africa. the Caribbean and South Asia* New Brunswick, N.J: Rutgers University Press.

Nwapa, Flora. 1966. *Efuru*, (Potsmouth, N.H.: Heinemann.

_____. 1970. *Idu* (Portsmouth, N.H.: Heinemann.

Owomoyela, Oyekan. 1979. African Literature an Introduction. Waltham, Mass.: Crossroads Press.

Robertson, Claire., Berger, Iris. 1986. *The Women and Class in Africa*. New York,N.Y.: African Publishing Co.

Stratton, Florence. 1994. Contemporary African Literature & the Politics of Gender. New York, N.Y.: Routeledg.

Sweetman, David. 1984. Women Leaders in African History (Portsmouth, N.H.: Heinemann.

Taiwo, Oladele. 1984. Female Novelists of Modern Africa (New York,N.Y.: St. Martin's Press.

Tetreault, Mary, Ann, Editor, 1994. *Women and Revolution in Africa Asia and the*

*New World* Columbia, S.C.: University of South Carolina.

Van Allen, Judith. "'Aba Riot' or Igbo 'Igbo Women'?" Ideology, Stratification, and the Invisibility of Women" cited in Hafkin et al. *Women in Africa: Studies in Social Science and Economic Change*.

# CHAPTER NINE

## Buchi Emecheta and the Politics of Gender

### Joya Uraizee

In many of her writings, Nigerian novelist Buchi Emecheta portrays the identity of the postcolonial Nigerian woman as fluid, or as one that displaces itself in various positions on a constantly evolving continuum. For her, identity is both subject to and created by the ideological history that surrounds it. As Pierre Macherey suggests, ideology is partly made up of those things that the text does not mention, that is, it operates silently, and its silences can be forced to speak (1978:132). Of course, the act of writing is, as Fredric Jameson points out, itself ideological (1981:79). Not only does the writer represent what Macherey calls a particular (class-based) ideology (1978:231), but the product itself creates a reaction within the reader or viewer, a reaction that Althusser terms "ideological self-recognition" (1990:156). This in turn implies that there will be confusion and contradiction in the way ideology operates, while the literary text seems to offer a symbolic or formal resolution of contradictions within itself. However, in Emecheta's writings, ideology reveals itself through gaps and absences, or a sense within her work of layers of contradictions, not all of which she seems able to control. These contradictions are most obvious with regard to the representation of people and events in Emecheta's narratives. In this chapter, I will discuss three aspects which reveal the contradictions most clearly: her focus on fragmented subjectivity and dialogic discourse; her preoccupation with gender differences; and her rather uncritical representation of middle class attitudes to social and economic structures. I will suggest that these three aspects show that Emecheta tends to subsume social and economic categorizations of Nigerian culture under one dominant mode: gender-based oppression. I will argue that for Emecheta, gender power controls and dominates political action in colonial and postcolonial Nigeria. Indeed, the postcolonial female subject becomes, in her writings, a figure that is constantly displaced or a voice that perpetually resists, within a social discourse that itself is evolving and shifting. By focusing on these preoccupations of hers, including the gaps and absences within them, I hope to reveal both the strengths and weaknesses of Emecheta's attempts to come to terms with the patriarchal ideology that surrounds her.

Emecheta's concern with questions of fragmented subjectivity or nationality and dialogic discourse seem to stem from her fractured sensibility as a writer and her sense of personal displacement. By this I mean that her writing suffers from a sense of fission in that the limitations imposed on her by history and ideology prompts her to silence or displace certain marginalized voices and issues while claiming to speak on their behalf. For example, her experiences with patriarchal oppression in Nigeria and economic self-sufficiency in England, frequently blinds her to sexual discrimination in England. She also seems somewhat isolated from mainstream Nigerian culture by virtue of her expatriate status.

In many of her novels, Emecheta uses a dialogic narrative structure in which many voices interact with each other. In her early novel, *The Bride Price* (1976), for example, there are several conflicting voices. The voice of literate, patriarchal authority is that of Okonkwo,[1] the village patriarch and Aku-nna's (the protagonist's) uncle, whose word is law, and who, with the help of his community, exerts a social and psychological hold over Aku-nna till her death. His voice is temporarily displaced by that of Chike, the village school teacher and son of slaves, who acts as Aku-nna's "redeemer," and helps her find temporary happiness and freedom. Ultimately, though, Chike is powerless to overcome the voice of authority that holds and paralyzes her. Aku-nna herself is a fragmented personality, and her voice is severely restricted. She seems to represent what Ernest Emenyonu calls "tortured and dehumanized womanhood" (1988:131), and speaks to us mainly through the voice of the third person narrator. Deeper in the shadows behind Aku-nna are the voices of her mother, Ma Blackie, and her brother, Nna-nndo, who are also dominated and silenced. Behind them are the nameless village women who appear in the discourse at varying levels of exploitation, working hard, bowing to tradition, and speaking occasionally not as individuals but as a collective. Again, behind these voices is that of a third person narrator who comments on the action at different stages and explains social and cultural customs and traditions to us. The final voice in the narrative is that of the oral story teller who recounts tales of the ancestors or of members of the community as examples of wisdom or as warnings to would-be rebels. This story-telling voice has no ancestral or prophesying power and no ability to influence the action. As Cynthia Ward suggests, this multiplicity of voices in the narrative is true "orality," that is, "multiple, often contradictory stories, fictions, realities, meanings-none being allowed to have precedence over the others without being marked as overtly coercive" (1990:87). Indeed, the narrative structure is interactive in that it highlights the idea that "just as an oral language cannot be separated from its speakers, in Ibuza [the place where the action unfolds], status, value, and self cannot be separated or alienated from the context that gives them significance: other people" (1990:94).

To take up just two of the voices, namely, the third person narrator and the oral storyteller, it is clear that the first functions as a voice of explanation, and the second, as a voice of authority. The third person narrator explains all the cultural customs and taboos of the community, but ends up erasing its own authority. This voice interrupts the narrative very frequently to explain actions or events, and the degree of explanation suggests that the listeners must know nothing about Ibuza culture. The voice comments on and explains Ibuza social interactions, family responsibilities, eating habits, mourning and death ceremonies, and marriage and fertility rituals. These descriptions are significant because, as Lloyd W. Brown points out, they appear in the text at the same time as Aku-Nna herself becomes aware of them, through a series of dramatic episodes (1981:50). This narrator also implies that its own voice is knowledgeable about both Ibuza customs and Western psychology. For example, in explaining why descendants of slaves were discriminated against in Ibuza, the narrator suggests that Ibuza culture itself is fairly new, and that "all the Ibuza people were immigrants; the *oshus* [slaves][2] just happened to be new immigrants" (1976:107). It then compares this phenomenon to that of the "very civilized peoples of America, Britain and Russia" (1976:107). This last statement has little irony, and is clearly being used to suggest that the narrative voice is well-informed about both Western psychology and history as well as Ibuza history and culture. Moreover, it suggests a rather uncritical depiction of the West as being the true seat of civilization, a depiction that frequently recurs in Emecheta's fiction.

Other customs the narrative voice speaks authoritatively about deal with sexual double standards and exploitation with a view to showing us how Aku-nna is ostracized for supposedly not being a virgin: "Anyone who contravened them [taboos and customs] was better dead. If you tried to hang on to life, you would gradually be helped towards death by psychological pressures. And when you were dead, people would ask: Did we not say so? Nobody goes against the laws of the land and survives" (1976:141). The idea is that patriarchal authority, tradition, and superstition, are really nothing more than "psychological pressures," that is, not repositories of ancient wisdom, but mind controlling devices. There is also a hint here that once this idea of mind control has been deciphered by the object of control, the psychological impact will be much less.

The narrative voice, then, is not really an authoritative voice at all, but rather a psychologizing voice of explanation. Behind it lies the final authority in the narrative-the power of the oral storyteller. Story telling voices intrude in the discourse at various points in the form of songs and stories about the Ibuza ancestors. Each story, however, emphasizes the artistry of the storyteller rather than the wisdom of the ancestors. The "pulsating groans," "mournful song[s]" and "repeated refrains" (1976:23) of the storytellers reveal only how the ancestors themselves must have sang and danced (1976:24). The final reference to story telling voices suggests that ultimately, it itself is the only voice that will prevail in Ibuza society: "Every girl born in Ibuza after Aku-nna's death was told her story to reinforce the old taboos of the land .... It was a psychological hold over every young girl that would continue to exist, even in the face of every modernization, until the present day. Why this is so is, as the saying goes, anybody's guess" (1976:168). Here the narrative voice and the discourse stop, leaving a void by the profession of ignorance and resignation. The suggestion is that after all the levels of displacement in the narrative, the last word goes to the oral storyteller whose art depends on interactive feedback from his or her listeners. This storyteller at the novel's end is a voice speaking for Okonkwo and tradition, and against Aku-nna and individualism. Curiously, though, it also makes Aku-nna into a kind of ancestor, that is, an ancestor who set a bad example because she married an *oshu*. Finally then, narrative power lies with that storyteller who can effectively frighten all prospective listeners into awe and obedience. All other voices must concede defeat.

This ending leaves us feeling dissatisfied, because, as Emenyonu points out, it describes all the problems of "African womanhood ... while firmly withholding a balm for its gaping sores" (1988:135). However, perhaps Emecheta is suggesting that the power to articulate Aku-nna's condition lies not in written, but in oral discourse. Indeed, the novel interweaves the various voices in such a way that we are led to expect a single powerful voice of authority to dominate and reveal itself at the end, but in each case that final revelation suggests an absence. Emecheta defers to an oral storyteller, but he or she has no power or ability to enforce his or her wisdom on others. This final negation of authority lies in part in the fact that Emecheta seems unable, due to the restrictions of class or gender, to sufficiently problematize the nature of that authority. Thus, we have a series of voices: Okonkwo, Chike, Aku-nna, Ma Blackie, and Nna-nndo; village women; third person narrator; oral storyteller; Emecheta and the listeners; one voice is constantly displacing and being displaced by the other.

Another example of Emecheta's preoccupation with fragmented subjectivity or nationality and dialogic discourse can be seen in a later novel, *Double Yoke* (1983). There are several layers to this narrative, too, and the main female character, Nko's, narrative involves a search for identity strung between the opposing poles of a career and domesticity, or, to use the narrator's words, tradition, and modernity. As a result, she seems unable to conceive of an existence as anything other than a choice between oppositional binaries. The most she can do is to try to be both at once, that is, "maneuver[ing] these men to give her both. They thought they could always call the tune and women like her must dance to it. With her, they were going to be wrong" (1983:135). In fact, what being both really means in the context of her narrative, is that pursuing a university degree leads to being doubly victimized, that is, being shunned by her fiancé and made pregnant by her professor. Rather belatedly, one of her friends advises her that a woman's identity need not always involve a choice between oppositional binaries, but could also include finding an existence that is independent of both: "It is easier to get a good degree using one's brain power than bottom power. They may try to tell you that your bottom power is easier and surer, don't believe them ... Nko, you don't have to lower yourself to that level. You are young, you're a beautiful girl. What's the matter with you?" (1983:155). Nko's temporary sense of independence at the end suggests that she is beginning to realize that she doesn't have to see her identity in terms of binaries, even if she does have a heavy yoke to carry. However, there is no narrative focus on that realization: it remains rather incomplete.

Perhaps Nko's inability to see her identity as anything other than a series of conflicting, oppositional selves stems from Emecheta's own ambivalent attitude towards tradition. For example, in an interview with Rolf Solberg, she stated that tradition is valuable and that "what is good in the old values-let us keep it. I wish not to look down on everything we have as bad or backward just because it is not modern" (1983:260). Yet in some of her novels, such as *The Slave Girl* and *The Joys of Motherhood,* she suggests that some traditional customs like slavery and polygyny are exploitative and should be discarded. In Nko's narrative, Emecheta seems to be suggesting that tradition traps the person who seeks the lure of Western individualism, so that she is oppressed by both individualism and tradition. What, then, is the way out of the trap? At the end of the novel, Nko is faced with both personal disgrace and family loss, without either a husband or a degree, and can only rely on a strong will to survive. However, whether that survival depends on Ete's (her fiancee's) support or not is left unresolved. As Barthelemy suggests, traditional culture does not "synchronize itself harmoniously to women; instead it returns to promote hardship and discord and to control female lives" (1989:569). Thus, Nko's search for an identity separate from that tradition, makes her oppressive situation even worse, and the only glimmer of hope is Ete's supposed change of heart. Whether that will provide Nko with a stronger sense of self-esteem is unclear.

A slightly different example of Emecheta's preoccupation with fragmented subjectivity or nationality can be seen in *Destination Biafra* (1982). Here the subjectivity of the nation is in question during the Nigerian Civil War (1967-70). The war is described as unfolding in a divided, fragmented and unnatural landscape in which dispossessed and desperate women hide.[3] In fact, the novel vividly depicts the plight of the African woman (and of women in general) trapped between two warring factions. The fragmentation of the land by Nigerian politicians and Western imperialists is actually a metaphor for the decay and degeneration of their minds. Thus, there is a lot of narrative focus on the constant formation and reformation of boundaries that enclose different kinds of spaces. For example, the boundaries enclosing and dividing Nigeria seem quite arbitrary, being dictated more by Western economic interests than a sense of identity among the people within it. As the protagonist, Debbie Ogedembge[4] realizes, "Nigeria was only one nation as a result of administrative balkanization by the British and French powers" (1982:175). In fact, national boundaries around Nigeria are drawn to ensure that the British neo-imperialists have control over the mineral deposits of the north and the oil in the east. And within this arbitrarily created space that is Nigeria, ethnic boundaries are used to subdivide regions. Ethnic boundaries are frequently used because, Emecheta suggests, ethnic or communal loyalties are stronger than a national identity. To the British, ethnic loyalties are a convenient lever for economic and political manipulation. The geographic locations of the various ethnic settlements within Nigeria are therefore used effectively in dividing up territory, yet these divisions change constantly depending on who is doing the dividing. President Brigadier Onyemere, for example, mixes up ethnic groups when he subdivides Nigeria, ostensibly to prevent each group from forming strong and aggressive political units. However, when Saka Momoh comes to power, he also mixes up ethnic groups and forms twelve states, but he claims this is necessary in order to protect the ethnic minorities: "Those silent minorities have to be considered. We had to create the twelve states to protect those people" (1982:124). However, Momoh's regrouping prompts Biafran leader Chijioke Abosi to break away from Nigeria because he (Abosi) realizes that Momoh's lines are drawn not to protect minorities but to "divide and rule. His [Momoh's] dividing the nation into twelve states would mean putting wedges between the united people of the Eastern Region, Abosi thought. And this must not be allowed to take place" (1982:106). Thus Abosi regroups Nigeria to make two separate countries, Nigeria and Biafra. The folly of this regrouping is noted by Debbie, a somewhat impartial participant in the war, because she points out that both Abosi and Momoh are really trying to keep the oil under their power, and that even if Biafra gives Abosi control over the oil, he cannot hope to win the war. She asks her lover, the Englishman Alan Grey: "how can a quarter of a nation fight the other three-quarters and win? It's sheer common sense" (1982:114). The only person who seems to accept the land as it is is Debbie's friend, Barbara Teteku, who argues that regardless of how arbitrarily colonial Nigeria's boundaries were drawn in the past, the Nigeria of the present should stick to those boundaries because Nigerian leaders need to "concentrate on making the way of living we are used to work, and not spend the little energy we have in destabilizing further our shaky nation" (1982:19). Thus, Nigeria as a geographic space becomes a site of contention and a locus of contradictory ideologies, and in this, it resembles Emecheta's notion of female subjectivity.

In fact, the exploitation of the female subject is Emecheta's second major narrative preoccupation. In many novels, her chief concern is to highlight gender differences in Nigerian/British society. She does so by pointing out how sexual oppression is linked to male control over a woman's body and to male domination of female labor and economic self-determination. However, it is curious that although she suggests that the dominance of African patriarchal systems oppress and silence African women of all classes, yet she tends to focus on individual males like Francis (in *Second Class Citizen*) or Okonkwo (in *The Bride Price*) as particularly brutal perpetrators of an oppressive system. The system itself is not, in many novels, critiqued.

In *Double Yoke*, for example, the narrative describes how Nko is a product of the past (traditional patriarchy)[5] but tries to adapt to the present (educational and social equality for women). Her attempts at self-definition suggest that women cannot remain rooted to the past if they want to achieve economic independence in the future; yet, their efforts to secure that independence lead only to abuse, exploitation, and pain in the present. For women like Nko, life in the present seems, in the words of Barthelemy, "mired in the past [and in] ... tradition; African culture provides no comfort, no haven. For women, patriarchal customs encourage antipathy to culture and tradition and intensify oppression" (1989:572). The overriding impression we get from her narrative is that despite individual

courage and perseverance, women are really powerless to initiate change, and that
only when men change their attitudes will real social change occur.

Nko frequently becomes a sex object to the men who control her life. As a
sex partner to Ete Kamba and Ikot, she is both passive and assertive, but overall,
passivity dominates. The first time she has sex with Ete, she allows him to do
what he wants, and also responds to his passion: "she allowed him, she gave in,
and she gave him all, her body yielding, responding to his demands, his thirst, his
hunger ... she was exhilarating, she was a bundle of soft, tender, warm flesh, very
young, very moist, not very difficult" (1983:52). In the second encounter, though,
she has just been beaten by Ete for supposedly not being a virgin. Confronted by
his rage, she tells him that her compliance was "my way of showing you that I
cared, that I was happy for your success ... I wanted to make it a full and happy
day for you. If that had cheapened me in your eyes, well I am sorry" (1983:58).
Although she seems self-effacing at this point, she does have the courage to claim
that men are to blame for women's sexual exploitation because "it takes two
people at least to make any woman a prostitute" (1983:58). After this, she lets him
have sex with her without enjoying it at all, just to make him happy, and remains
withdrawn and cynical, fitting the stereotype of receptacle that Ete views her as:
"it did not matter to her one way or the other what Ete Kamba had done with her
body. She [was] ... passive and still" (1983:60).

Her behavior is very similar when her professor, the Rev. Elder Ikot, rapes
her. Knowing she is in his power, she turns herself into a "wooden doll" and lets
him "have what he wanted" (1983:140). Yet afterwards, she asserts herself
enough to threaten him with scandal if he doesn't make sure she gets a "first class
honours degree" (1983:140). Finally, when she has sex with Ikot again just before
Ete beats him up, she walks into his room with her head held high like a "proud
criminal," but walks out "like somebody who had completely rejected herself"
(1983:149). Even then, she has the strength to assert herself to respond to Ete's
taunts by accusing him of hypocrisy. Telling herself that she has nothing more to

lose, she refuses to let Ete make her feel guilty.

Nko's constant shuttling between passivity and self-assertion marks all her activities. She herself never quite provides all the answers to her motivation, and we are frequently left guessing. She suddenly transforms herself from a quiet and loving village girl to a worldly-wise woman who believes in "bottom power" and we can only sense that this is because she wants "both worlds" that is, being both "academician" and "quiet nice and obedient wife" (1983:94). However, when she is presented with both, she feels obliged to choose only one. The only reason the narrator gives for her determination to get her degree even when it means prostituting herself is her conviction that she cannot go back to her family and admit that she dropped out because she wanted to be a faithful wife. She seems bound by the need to help her family rise out of poverty by getting a degree, but she also wants to prove to the world that "what a man could do, a woman could do also" (1983:107). Yet the novel closes without her proving anything of the sort, so the overall impression is one of female helplessness and passivity.

Another example of Emecheta's focus on male control over female bodies appears in *Destination Biafra,* in which the soldiers on both sides of the civil war are described as being very aggressive towards any women caught in their path. In fact, the main action of the narrative as far as Debbie is concerned, is made up of her encounters with cruel men. Despite her father's money and her own education and sophistication, Debbie is raped and disgraced in the war, not once, but several times. Here, Emecheta's point seems to be that women are always victims in a war, regardless of whether they are rich or poor. Debbie's experiences with rape and disgrace are central to the action of the novel.

Before she is raped the first time, Debbie finds out that women of all ethnic backgrounds are constantly being beaten or raped or abused, usually by soldiers whose commanders refuse to accept responsibility for these actions. Instead, the soldiers claim that "'It is war, and in a war situation men lose their self-control,' as if that were explanation enough" (1982:119). Even the worst atrocities against women go unpunished, and pregnant women are cut open and their beheaded fetuses are left lying on the roads; captured women of all ages are stripped and then squeezed and poked by enemy soldiers at all times of day or night; and murdered women are regarded as war statistics and are rarely accounted for.

In one scene, Debbie is gang raped by a group of crude Nigerian soldiers when she is on the road to Asaba to try and persuade Abosi to surrender. Having stopped her car outside Ibadan to help a poor Ibo man and his sickly, pregnant wife, she is then faced by their ridicule toward her army uniform and gun. They refuse to believe that she is really an officer, and neither do the Nigerian soldiers who suddenly pounce on them from nowhere. After shooting the men, stripping Debbie's mother and cutting up the pregnant woman, they gang rape Debbie till she becomes unconscious. After this experience, all her will and determination vanishes, and she alternately wants to die or hang her head in shame. Her self-respect completely disappears when she hears the casual attitude of the Biafran soldiers who rescue her: "hundreds of women have been raped-so what? It's war. She's lucky to be even alive. She'll be all right" (1982:135). As she realizes bitterly, she has been made a victim by the very people she had been trying to help, the Nigerian side, and that no self-respecting bourgeois Nigerian or Biafran man would desire her after she has been raped by poor, Black Nigerian soldiers. Her final humiliation comes when her mother consoles her with the advice that this is the "fate of all women" (1982:157).

Debbie is severely battered by this attack, both physically and mentally, and realizes that "in the eyes of the world ... she was a tarnished woman" (1982:159). Yet she gets her will to survive back when she realizes that the Nigerian army is continuing its genocidal campaign against the Ibos, and that the only way to stop it is to get Abosi to surrender. So she sets off alone towards the east and, after many misadventures, is almost raped again. This time, she is captured by Nigerian soldiers while travelling in a bus full of Ibo refugees, heading toward Asaba. The Nigerian soldiers strip the women and interrogate the men and Debbie is brought in front of the commander, Lawal Salihu, her one-time colleague. Taunting her for proving herself a poor soldier and a weak woman he boasts that by raping her, he will show her that she is "nothing but a woman" (1982:75). The only reason he spares her is because she confesses that she has already been raped by ordinary soldiers. Seeing his confusion and disgust, she taunts him with ridicule:

> Allah will never forgive you now because you tried to violate a woman who has been raped by so many soldiers, a woman who may now be carrying some disease, a woman who has been raped by black Nigerian soldiers. You thought you were going to use a white man's plaything, as you called me, only to realize that you held in your arms a woman who has slept with soldiers. (1982:176)

The irony is that Lawal, and later, Grey, both react with horror at having touched a woman who has been raped by common Black men. Debbie realizes bitterly that they would probably have been less disgusted if white men had raped her. Strangely, then, she escapes rape through rape, so that rape itself becomes symbolic for all male aggression and power. Just as men parcel up and destroy the land, so too, they destroy their compassion for women. The point, then, of all these descriptions of violated female bodies is to show that male greed for money and power makes them little better than animals. By treating women and children as subhuman objects to be devoured and destroyed, the men cease to be human.

Men who are cruel to the point of becoming inhuman appear in *Second Class Citizen* (1975), too. Here, however, the main problem being analyzed is not civil war but male domination of female labor and economic self-determination among upper class or elite[6] expatriate Nigerians. The protagonist, Adah, despite being very strong-willed, cannot escape being objectified by her husband, Francis, who regards all women as commodities[7] that are "bought and paid for and must remain like that, silent obedient slaves" (1975:156). She is subjected to deliberate and cruel abuse from Francis. Because he values her only for her salary, he does not even bother to express any humane feelings for her, and accuses her of failing as a wife and mother when she stops working due to ill health. His sadistic oppression is based on capitalist and patriarchal principles, by which he "was the male, and he was right to tell her what she was going to do. Adah, from the day of her registry marriage, had seen the romantic side of her life being shattered, like broken glass, about her" (1975:28). Instead of marriage and sex being a process of learning and a means of communication, they become the source of her physical and sexual exploitation. As Katherine Frank has pointed out, the real "second class citizenship [she experiences] ... derives far more from Adah's anatomy than from the colour of her skin" (1982:492). To use Ketu Katrak's words, "the economic oppression of woman-as-slave [is] represented by Emecheta literally, in the institution of slavery, and metaphorically, in the institution of marriage-the woman in both cases is owned, body and soul" (1987:165).

One of the main points being made in this novel is that in Ibo society, women of all classes are often commodified into producers of male children and bringers of large bride prices. Indeed, Emecheta seems to be arguing that patriarchal oppression in Africa in general is primarily economic. For Adah, then, sex and marriage becomes an endless grind of hard work, continuous cycles of pregnancy and sickness, and physical and mental abuse. The only way she can communicate with Francis is through providing him with sex and money, and she soon learns to manipulate him with these. She begins to deny him sex until he agrees to take some responsibility for their housing, and she also withholds money until he begins to contribute some, too. Finally, she gives up on marriage as a means of communication when she realizes that:

> ... she was not loved, and was being used to give
> Francis an education ... she had only begun to love
> and care for him later. But the love was short-lived
> because Francis did nothing to keep it alive. She felt
> she was being betrayed ... she so wished she could
> tell her worries to someone ... Since there was no

one to tell, she had to put on a cloak of indifference.
(1975:126)

All this oppression leaves such an impression on her that even when she finally chooses to leave Francis she is overcome not by relief but by loneliness: "she cried then. She was lonely again, just as when Pa died and Ma married again and she had to live in a relative's house" (1975:147). All she has with her in her new-found freedom at the end is "four babies, her new job and a box of rags" (1975:171) together with a painful conscience. As Frank suggests, she cannot "shrug off years of conditioning that have inculcated wifely subservience to one's husband" (1982:493). The final vestiges of her self-esteem disappear when she is completely disowned by the very husband she worked as a slave for, and her economic independence is undercut by the fact that she has no child support or monetary help from him: "To him [Francis] Adah and the kids ceased to exist. Francis told her this ... [and also said] `I don't mind their [the kids] being sent for adoption'" (1975:174). As a woman, wife, and mother, this is the cruelest form of exile, and Adah is left trying to cope with it. This ending of the novel shows Emecheta's dual concern with the biological and economic control over women within patriarchal and capitalist postcolonial Nigeria (and in England), and how one form of control, in Katrak's words, often reinforced the other (1987:159).

Patriarchal and capitalist control over Nigerian women seems to be the principle upon which the university that Nko attends in *Double Yoke* is based. At first, the university fosters a kind of individualism that seems, on the surface, to be a great benefit to both men and women because it involves a reformist way of thinking and insists on a rejection of customs that have become obsolete. Thus, a woman at the university can reject traditional taboos against female education and get a "new self" (1983:92). She can question everything, even at the risk of male disapproval, and can develop her own defenses against male exploitation. However, the narrative also suggests that the university offers individualism and competition at a cost, namely, the risk of becoming commodified and objectified.

The university slowly begins to look, therefore, like a structure based on hierarchies imposed by class and gender, which can oppress women even more powerfully than village patriarchy. In fact, it becomes an institution of capitalist male oppression.

The university is actually a microcosm of society because it is dominated by affluent males like Professor Ikot. Ikot is described as a religious hypocrite who uses religious rhetoric and economic status to enslave male students and sexually exploit female ones. Deriving most of his power from patriarchal tradition, he seems able to commodify his students into objects of mental and physical control. He treats female students like Nko as sex objects, using his words and body language to suggest to them that "if you don't let me sleep with you at any time I feel like it, you don't get your degree. Period!" (1983:139). Overall, he seems completely unscrupulous and depraved, and the university he controls creates confusions and contradictions by mixing up traditional and Western forms of oppression. This suggests that suffering will not be eradicated when one form of oppression is removed, since various forms combine to oppress individuals. Overall, the narrative seems to suggest that gender relations in postcolonial Nigeria are based on one-sided exploitation, in that women are continually abused by patriarchal and Western social systems. The implication is that only when the individual has the strength to discard the taboos and superstitions enforced by tradition can he or she experience true freedom.

Emecheta's third main preoccupation is, I would argue, also a limitation in that she confines herself to the ideology of the Western educated bourgeois class of urban Nigeria. Most of the voices that speak to us from her books reflect the ideologies of this class. As a result, she only partially critiques the basis of that class's hegemony in her own particular society; nor does she seem aware of the hegemonic function of her own voice within that class.

For example, in *Destination Biafra* she does make an attempt to describe the suffering of the dispossessed peasant and working class women on both sides of the war. Yet, her protagonist, and therefore, her focus, is on an upper class woman, Debbie. The peasant women become the real casualties of the war while Debbie learns from their experiences. The peasant women witness the brutal deaths of their husbands and children; see their homes destroyed; and roam about in the forests and remote villages in order to stay alive. Rather than presenting them as rugged individualists, Emecheta presents them as long-suffering survivors, thereby showing that in this war, as in other wars before it, the vulnerable sections of society suffer the most. Moreover, in this war, the women are defeated not just by the machines of war (guns and bullets), but also by the agents of war (male politicians and soldiers). They suffer starvation, rape and mutilation by whichever side they happen to fall foul of. As one Ibo peasant woman tells a Biafran soldier, they will no longer help either side because they are "tired of being in the middle. Your Biafran soldiers killed our men and raped our girls, because you accused us of harbouring enemy soldiers, then Nigerian soldiers would accuse us of the same thing even though we were innocent. There was nobody to protect us so we formed our own militia" (1982: 230-231). As Debbie realizes when she travels with them, "the real war is being fought here" (1982:231).

Indeed, although Debbie emerges at the end of the novel as the hope for a different future, the hope for change is undermined by the fact that she is clearly implicated in the bourgeois system herself. At the end, she claims that she is "a woman and a woman of Africa. I am a daughter of Nigeria and if she is in shame, I shall stay and mourn with her in shame" (1982:258). Yet, she belongs to the same bourgeois class as the politicians who fueled the war and therefore cannot help being subject to their ideology. She even sleeps with a white man (Alan Grey) despite despising his politics, and before the war, only made half-hearted attempts to protest social injustice. For example, she complains that rich Nigerians show off their wealth too ostentatiously at parties, but wears gold framed shoes herself just to please her father. As Chidi Amuta points out, most

novels written about the Nigerian Civil War reflect the ideology and attitudes of
the bourgeoisie, yet often the protagonists of such novels are critical of or
opposed to these values (1984:61). He concludes that although the Nigerian war
novel was "inspired by the hegemonic ideology of the bourgeoisie" it often
became quite critical of and even hostile to "the position, interests and role(s) of
that class" (1984:61). In this regard, Emecheta does not seem to be as critical of
bourgeois values as the other novelists Amuta mentions, and nowhere does she
suggest that one of the chief reasons for the failure of African independence is the
failure of elite leadership of the bourgeoisie. The furthest she does go is to suggest
that the bourgeois leaders are puppets of the West, and are therefore complicitous
in the carnage of the war. In fact, throughout the middle section of the novel
Debbie seems to be just "slumming it" for a while with the Ibo peasant women,
and she returns at the end to her elite status and escapes from the suffering
masses. Nor are the suffering masses, despite their resilience, the central focus of
the novel; instead, it is Debbie's realization that she is not one of them: "as she
[Debbie] walked down that dry road in that heat, with the weight of the child
almost breaking her back, it struck her that African women of her age carried
babies like this all day and still farmed and cooked; all she had to do now was
walk, yet she was in such pain. What kind of African woman was she, indeed?"
(1982:191). In fact, I would agree with Amuta's conclusion that like most other
Nigerian war novels, this one too, indicts only the "*quality* of bourgeois
leadership, not the *basis* of that hegemony" (1984:69). This throws into confusion
the optimism of novel's ending, because it suggests that the agency of change,
Debbie, is complicitous with the cause of the problem, the corrupt leaders, being
of the same class as them. Finally, then, a possible way to get rid of that
hegemony that is not explored in the novel, would be to empower the strong-
willed peasant women whose plight Debbie temporarily shares, since they display
the determination to survive; can adapt to a world destroyed by, and emptied of,
powerful men; and are not completely controlled by the bourgeois ideology of the

politicians.

Perhaps Emecheta's oblivion to the hegemonic function of her own upper class voice within Nigeria arises partly out of her acquisition of a reading public and a critical following in the West. In this context, she tends to present subaltern[8] or peasant discourse as extremely marginalized, fragmented and effaced. In *The Bride Price*, for example, Aku-nna is a subaltern not because of her social class, but because of her gender. She is static and homogenized, silenced, and sexually violated. Her marriage against social customs brings, on herself and her family, social disgrace, exile, and death. In much of the narrative she stands bewildered, in Oladele Taiwo's words, at a "cultural crossroads" (1984:107), enslaved by what Frank calls traditional rules and taboos (1982:483). Under male scrutiny, she appears insecure and silent, her main distinguishing feature being, according to the narrator, "gentle helplessness" and silence (1976:119). Hers is a fragmented personality and the first view of her in the text is that of someone who is lost. In Lagos, the one person who seems to understand her is her father, but when he dies, she is left "frightened" and "hypnotized" (1976:12), grief stricken, and disoriented. These fears arise because without a man, a family is thought to be lost. As the third person narrator explains, "a fatherless family is ... a family without shelter ... in fact a non-existing family" (1976:28). Part of Aku-nna's feelings of being lost arises from the fact that she is very insecure through most of the novel. Thus, when she moves back to Ibuza from Lagos, she and her brother become even more confused, like "helpless fishes caught in a net; they could not as it were, go back into the sea, for they were trapped fast, and yet they were still alive because the fisherman was busy debating within himself whether it was worth killing them to take home, seeing as they were such small fry" (1976:82). In fact, Aku-nna never properly adjusts to all the social rituals and taboos of Ibuza, becoming confused and unhappy, or, in Chike's words, "afraid of her own people" (1976:82). The only person she can depend on is Chike, and she ends up leaning on him so much that when he considers leaving

Ibuza without her, she feels devastated: "if he left, left her here alone in this town, she would be heartbroken. She would be lost, like the ants without their tracks" (1976:91).

Another distinguishing feature of Aku-nna as subaltern is her loneliness. In one scene, she breaks down in school, sits under a tree, and reflects on her lonely life. She counts off all the people she needs who are not there for her, including her father, mother and brother, and concludes: "It came to Aku-nna clearly now that she was completely alone" (1976:89). She seems unable to communicate, so that she thinks that even if she had their attention, she would not be able to explain any clear reasons to them as to why she feels so unhappy. Chike provides solace and companionship both before and after she marries him, and her feelings of loneliness do subside then. However, even after her marriage, she remains insecure and is troubled by feelings of guilt and depression. Rather than making the most of her companionship and prosperity, she becomes afraid and begins to hear voices. The voices she hears are those of her own people, condemning her for her unpaid bride price, and this alarms her so much that she is afraid to be by herself after a while: "Over and over again, she heard this voice calling her, telling her she must come back to her family, to her people" (1976:163). Only Chike and his father are able to rationalize that the voices are not real, but are actually psychological pressures imposed on her by the weight of custom. But the fact that social custom has such a hold over her suggests that she has been indoctrinated into believing and fearing taboos and warnings. Fear, then, is the key behind these customs, the narrator suggests, and "that was the intention behind all the taboos and customs. Anyone who contravened them was better dead" (1976:141). These powerful voices seem to "suck her blood" till she dies in labor due to weakness induced by anemia. As Brown suggests, she literally "dies of the fear that the curse will be effective, and on this basis her death flows from the novel's central thesis: that fate or destiny in its most significant sense is not based on the mysterious predispositions of inscrutable supernatural forces, but on the function of social institutions and the shaping patterns of cultural traditions" (1981:49).

Part of the reason why Aku-nna is so passive in the face of all this oppression is because she is silenced and unable to articulate the terms of her oppression. She speaks only through absence because she is quiet by nature, and because, in Ward's words, her inner voice or *chi* needs a respondent in order to be able to communicate (1990:88). Even when she is happy she seldom talks, a condition which to her relatives seems unnatural and eerie, but which the narrator explains was a result of her desire to "listen to [her] ... heart" (1976:105). Self-expression seems to overwhelm her, and without a voice, her real sorrow remains within her, oppressing her with its weight or "heaviness [which] she used to feel when carrying a load of firewood. Tears would not even come" (1976:37). One could conclude that her abilities to articulate her status as subaltern are limited. Even questioning it seems difficult, given the discouragement she experiences about asking too many questions. Faced with no outlet to vent her anxieties, she retreats into submissiveness that translates as a preference for death over retaliation against abuse. What makes Aku-nna's silence even more significant is the fact that her *chi* is also stifled and oppressed. At the end of the novel, her *chi* is completely erased by Okonkwo's, accusing her of betrayal. Clearly, then, Emecheta tends to represent subaltern or lower class voices as completely suppressed.

Besides her presentation of subaltern discourse as extremely marginalized, Emecheta's representation of the various class positions in Nigerian society is invariably oppositional; and her discourse always reverts to a depiction of the social injustice and sexual inequality that result from a rigid adherence to the rituals of African patriarchy. Even then, her depiction of that patriarchy is not always accurate. For example, an "alternate" world [9] of freedom and equality is visualized in *Double Yoke,* and it is based on a form of sexual equality that is achievable through a delicate balance between the rival claims of tradition and modernism. In order to achieve this balance, the narrative suggests, both men and women must have the strength to support social change, and to fight abuse. More specifically, it means that men must change their attitudes towards women and regard them with respect and understanding, and as individuals in their own right, even if this change requires opposing traditional practices. The alternate world therefore involves notions of gender relations that are at odds with the traditional practices that the novel describes. However, the alternate world in this novel is not really achievable.

The alternate world which is unachievable is described at various points by Miss Bulewao, the creative writing instructor, who, the narrator tells us, represents modernity. Bulewao is presented as something of an anomaly in the university community because she conceptualizes a world in which the problems of the conflicting claims of patriarchy and modernism are solved. The solution she provides seems to be a simple replacement of patriarchal taboos by freedom for women to be socially independent. The positing of such a solution at the end of the narrative is problematic, and it is made more so because it over-simplifies the social problems facing postcolonial Nigerian women. It over-simplifies because it suggests that freedom for women can be initiated by actually writing changes into the individual's psyche. In one scene, therefore, Bulewao has her students write a creative description of "how you would like your ideal Nigeria to be" (1983:5). Her students are all male, and one of them, Ete, decides to respond by writing about his history, which becomes interwoven with Nko's. At the end, Bulewao tells her students that "only men with large hearts can love and understand. That does not make them weak. It makes them great" (1983:162). The implication is that when men change their attitudes and learn to respect women as individuals, both they, and the nation, will achieve greatness. It also suggests that women do not need to change in this way because they have already internalized this greatness. Or it could mean that the only social power that women have is to influence men to follow their own way of thinking, and that only when men change, will the politics of gender also change.

On this note of muted optimism, the narrative ends, and we are left with the impression that it takes a special kind of person to be able to visualize and internalize social change in the Nigeria of the future. In fact, however, all this suggestion of change is no change at all, because it does not imply any alteration to the power structure that causes oppression (the patriarchy). Women are not empowered to carve their own identities and the power to dictate change remains firmly in male hands. At best, female power in the narrative is the power of survival, that is, the power to keep on struggling. As Emecheta once said in an interview with Rolf Solberg, "our problem is beyond feminism ... men ... are not free themselves, even in the so-called independent states. They cannot see that they are being used. So until they are free you cannot really ... claim to be a feminist" (1983:260).

However, in consistently reducing the politics of gender to a struggle between traditional patriarchy and modern individualism, the narrative over-simplifies the nature of female oppression in postcolonial Nigeria. The fact that individualism (and by implication, capitalism) can doubly oppress the postcolonial Nigerian woman is not sufficiently elaborated. That is, although the narrative establishes that patriarchy and individualism act together to form a double oppression, it does not follow that this can be resolved or altered by a simple reversal, as the narrative would have it. Change, according to the narrative, means replacing patriarchy with the power of individuals in competition with one another, whereas in fact both situations are often equally repressive. As Ketu Katrak has shown, capitalist style individualism often reinforced patriarchal forms of oppression (1987:159), and therefore both joined together to control women (1987:160). Alternatively, capitalism and patriarchy often oppressed women by working in tandem, as Sangari and Vaid have shown. According to them, both tradition and modernity in India have been "carriers of patriarchal ideologies ... [and are] colonial constructs" (1990:17). The same argument could be applied to

Nigeria, where, as Katrak suggests, "capitalism and patriarchy have joined hands to control women" (1987:160), with the result that postcolonial Ibo women became dominated by men economically, politically, and socially. Whatever few political rights women were given under African patriarchy were taken away by capitalism or colonialism so that "postcolonial Capitalist society in Nigeria landed Igbo [sic] women with different forms of oppression [without changing] ... any of the institutions" of oppression already in place (1987:163). Therefore, despite gaining access to education and modern ideas of individualism, women remain on the margins of political and economic power (1987:160). In such a context, replacing traditional taboos with modern individualism will not do away with oppression. Instead, a valorization of worthwhile customs from patriarchal and capitalist traditions might provide some kind of hope for a future of freedom.

Another example of Emecheta's problematic treatment of class relations that reverts to a simplified analysis of sexual inequality occurs in *Second Class Citizen*. Adah is presented frequently as an intellectual who exhibits typical middle class attitudes about wealth and status in post-independence Nigeria, especially the necessity of going to the U.K. and becoming a "family of Ibo elites" (1975:25) on their return. Yet she remains an elite only after a tremendous struggle which involves alienation and a withdrawal from family and communal relations. At the end of her struggles she emerges a battered and miserable survivor. Katherine Frank calls her a "liberated, self-sufficient heroine" (1982:478), but I would argue that her liberation is more symbolic than real. In fact, Frank regards Adah's feminist aspirations and her African aspirations as mutually opposed throughout the novel, so that in order to maintain a free existence, she has to continue to live in the West (1982:492). This is an over-simplified approach to Adah's struggle.

However, despite this weakness, the novel does provide valuable insights on the ways in which racial, sexual, and class-based oppression are inextricably linked within a culture, so that one kind of oppression often leads to another. For example, the narrator tells us that living in a "white" society like England somehow brings out all the worst aspects of Nigerian class and race prejudice. Thus, working class Nigerian women become so manipulated by their racist environment in London that they do not even realize how oppressed they are: "As soon as a Nigerian housewife in England realized that she was expecting a child ... she would advertise for a foster-mother. No one cared whether a woman was suitable or not, no one wanted to know whether the house was clean or not; all they wanted to be sure of was that the foster mother was white. The concept of whiteness could cover a multitude of sins" (1975:46).

As the ending of the novel makes clear, even elite women fail to make much headway against these internalized and exterior prejudices. On the social level, neither the problems of Nigerian patriarchy nor those of Western capitalism, especially those pertaining to the exploitation of women for sex or money, are resolved, they continue to exist. On the personal level, Adah is not really empowered in any way except by her ability to write; instead she is left alone and without legal and communal support. The underlying metaphor of this and other Emecheta novels, then, is that womanhood is, as Frank puts it, "a condition of victimization and servitude" (1982:479), and freedom or free will is hard to attain. And this concept is further complicated by the fact that Emecheta frequently invokes the West as a haven of freedom for women, while suggesting that Africa is a continuous grind of oppression. Therefore, despite her best efforts, Adah is always defined in terms of the exploitation she experiences, and not on her own terms.

Having described above some of Emecheta's ambivalences with regard to her presentation of class and gender relations, I would like to point out that she does, occasionally, critique the role that western imperialism has played in creating some of these imbalances. In *Destination Biafra,* for example, she suggests that independence has brought Nigeria not peace and prosperity, but neo-imperialism, political corruption, and genocide. Emecheta's point seems to be that

Nigerian independence is quite meaningless unless it is economic as well as political. She shows how dangerous it is to have rulers who are just puppets serving Western economic interests rather than the needs of the people. Indeed, this is the most anti-imperialist of Emecheta's novels because here she definitely questions Western values and philosophies. She implies that the only hope for Nigeria in the future is the strength and will of upper class Nigerian women who emerge as the battered boundary markers of freedom at the end.

Incidents that take place in the past explain how the British imperialists viewed Nigerian independence as a means to assert economic control while abrogating political and administrative responsibilities. As the last British governor-general, MacDonald, points out just before the official ceremony granting independence takes place, "All independence will give them [Nigerians] is the right to govern themselves. That has nothing to do with whom they trade with" (1982:7). Trading partners are important to the British because they fear that independence will give Nigerians the confidence to strike deals with the Soviets and others regarding the drilling or extraction of Nigeria's vast deposits of crude oil. So even before the first free Nigerian election takes place, MacDonald and his advisers decide to use "proportional representation" as the voting principle. In doing so, they hope to ensure that the Hausa, who are the largest ethnic group in Nigeria, and, in their opinion, "ignorant and happy in their ignorance" (1982:6), will "rule forever" (1982:7). Even before the election campaigning begins, the British imperial government secretly backs the Hausa candidates; private British companies fund Yoruba candidates; while the candidates themselves campaign erratically. The only Nigerian politician with any awareness of national issues is Dr. Ozimba, the Ibo party candidate, who, despite his experience as a political activist in the past, is unaware of the political maneuvers taking place around him. He seems to have a definite ideology (Pan-Africanism, one Nigeria), but is no match for the imperial manipulators. Clearly, the British imperial government is motivated by greed, because their credo is that "any profit to come out of Nigeria should go to Britain rather than to other countries .... [they] did not want to see the poor of the country poorer through power being handed to a few greedy politicians" (1982:26). The hypocrisies in this statement are obvious, besides which it is false. The money does stay in the hands of greedy politicians, only they are British, not Nigerian. Overall, then, this account of the background to the first election suggests that it was a time of economic inequality and political injustice.

In the narrative, Nigerian society and its political system are characterized by betrayal and hypocrisy resulting from "indirect rule" and "divide and rule." As regards indirect rule, the narrative shows how proportional representation enables the British puppet, Mallam Nguru Kano, a Hausa politician, to take over as first Prime Minister of independent Nigeria, even though he has no contact with the realities of Nigerian politics. More importantly, this policy causes dissatisfaction and unrest in the country because the average Nigerian believed that Dr. Ozimba would be first Prime Minister. As one Ibo soldier complains, "Mallam Nguru Kano the first Prime Minister indeed! This result is like playing *Hamlet* without the prince" (1982:25). Kano, being a member of the feudal Muslim elite, and leader of a people the British have favored with the top positions in the military, allows the British imperial government to maintain economic control over Nigeria. Thus, independence is really valid only "on paper" (1982:24). Also, as Debbie realizes, this control is likely to remain in place for a long time, so that the neo-imperialists may "rule the country indirectly forever" (1982:42). Most of the novel's narrative attention is directed toward showing how the neo-imperialist policies of post-independence Nigeria led to so many tensions that they finally erupted into civil war.

Thus, the novel depicts post-revolutionary Nigerian society gripped by a crisis that results in horror rather than hope. Emecheta stresses the need for economic change as a primary condition for the revolution to be successful. She argues her case by depicting horror and betrayal, thereby underscoring the urgent need for action. Finally, she views the postcolonial Nigerian woman as reflective of both the social ills as well as the cure. Her novel implies that women must begin the process of change by internalizing their own versions of social and economic equality.

## CONCLUSION

In conclusion, Emecheta's narrative representation of the various gender and class relations in society is invariably oppositional rather than dialogic. This constant opposition is presented in the form of various voices and narratives which continually "interrupt" each other to produce what looks suspiciously like a master narrative. Emecheta's master narrative is, in fact, what she perceives as the social injustice and sexual inequality that result from a rigid adherence to the rituals of African patriarchy. Even then, her depiction of that patriarchy is, as I have shown, not always accurate. The main inaccuracies lie in her persistence in treating social ills as individual failings that deviate from or disregard the capitalist system; and in her tendency to set up Africa and the West as binary opposites representing stagnation and dynamism. As I have indicated above, while she suggests that the dominance of African patriarchal systems oppress and silence women of all classes and races, she tends to focus on individual males like Francis (who unfortunately degenerates into a caricature), as particularly brutal perpetrators of an oppressive system.

Nevertheless, Emecheta's intervention within postcolonial fiction is valuable primarily because she connects postcolonial feminine identity to the institutionalized nature of traditional, patriarchal oppression. Although her focus is more on the representation of sexual oppression, than on alternatives to victimization, she does give the postcolonial female a voice. Unfortunately, her female voices seem unable to speak except in total opposition to male discourse (as is the case with Nko and Adah). Ultimately, though, she seems to imply that postcolonial female discourse arises out of the contradictions and clashes within traditional patriarchy and Western capitalism.

Moreover, the overall implications of Emecheta's approaches to race and ethnicity are very important. In her novels, she seems to advocate a thorough Westernization of Nigerian patriarchy, and in some places, suggests that male oppression of female bodies and labor is more prevalent in Black males than in whites (for example, at one point, the narrator of *Second Class Citizen* claims Francis' race makes him unable to change his oppressive and chauvinistic behavior toward Adah). Yet at the same time she repudiates white racism as she experiences it in Britain, especially if its perpetrators are lower class whites. Only occasionally, as in *Destination Biafra*, does she critique Western nations directly.

Thus, Emecheta's writings suggest that gender power controls and dominates political action. What this implies for the nature of postcolonial political fiction is that narrative voice and political identity are in a state of flux. The postcolonial woman becomes a figure that is constantly displaced or a voice that constantly resists, within a discourse that is evolving and shifting. She is at once elite and powerless, at once subversive and exploitative.

## NOTES

1     Note that this name is an echo of the central character of Chinua Achebe's *Things Fall Apart* and therefore seems to signal a move on Emecheta's part to rewrite Ibo women back into a reconstructed Ibo history that Achebe, in fact, wrote them out of. However, Aku-nna's inability to cope with the restrictions Okonkwo places on her suggests that the two histories are not very different.

2     The Ibo concept of slave is fairly complex. The *osu* or *oshu* were, according to Robert M. Wren, the lowest of the three ranks of Ibo society. Above them were the slaves and the freeborn. An *osu* could not rise into the other ranks, and, together with his descendants, was doomed to his social stigma forever. The other ranks could, however, fall into the rank of *osus*. Despite their lowly status, *osus* could farm, raise families, and collect titles. Many of them were sent to school and to the church for education and careers (1980:40).

3     For a more extensive discussion of the nature of the fragmented national boundaries as they appear in *Destination Biafra* see my article entitled "Fragmented Borders and Female Boundary Markers in Buchi Emecheta's *Destination Biafra*" in an upcoming issue of *The Journal of the Midwest Modern Language Association*.

4     Debbie's name suggests that she is a cultural hybrid because it is both Western (Debbie) and Nigerian (Ogedembge).

5     Patriarchy, as defined by Gerda Lerner, is an institutionalized form of male dominance over women and children, both within the family and in society in general. It suggests that men hold the powerful positions in important social institutions, while women do not, although women are not entirely deprived of all rights (economic, legal, and political). It takes various forms and modes in different societies and adapts itself in different

Traffic in Women" which traces the ways in which political and psychoanalytical philosophers have perpetuated the exploitation of women. Discussing Marx, Lacan, Freud and others, Rubin points out that women have been commodified as a reserve labor force for capitalism (1975:160), are part of the process of reproduction of labor (1975:162), and function as a basic form of gift exchange (1975:173), among others.

8    Gayatri C. Spivak borrows the term "subaltern" from Antonio Gramsci, for whom the subaltern was the repressed peasant, and suggests that it is an intellectually and politically loaded term, functionally oppositional to "dominant" or "elite" (1988:1). As regards the subaltern woman, Spivak suggests that she is a figure that moves from clan to clan as "daughter/sister and wife/mother [and who] syntaxes patriarchal continuity even as she is herself drained of proper identity" (1988:31). Thus, her consciousness cannot be fully recovered (1988:12) because its interpreters are always subject to the ideology of the elite and it is always "askew from its received signifiers ... it is effaced even as it is disclosed" (1988:11). Indeed, such a woman "disappears" into what Spivak calls "a violent aporia between subject and object status" (1988:306). Since, she argues, the subaltern male cannot express himself in terms that are understood by the imperialist, then the subaltern female is "even more deeply in shadow" (1988: 287) and is mute. In addition, the very terms of her existence are dictated to her by the oppressor and this implicates her in her own oppression.

9    Many postcolonial novels are concerned with visions of alternate worlds characterized by freedom and equality, faith, and security. These alternate or possible worlds are made real in the minds of the postcolonial subjects by a kind of internalization of concepts of race, class, and gender that are at odds with the neo-colonial world that surrounds them. Thus, the subjects create alternative histories and identities for themselves that set

Traffic in Women" which traces the ways in which political and psychoanalytical philosophers have perpetuated the exploitation of women. Discussing Marx, Lacan, Freud and others, Rubin points out that women have been commodified as a reserve labor force for capitalism (1975:160), are part of the process of reproduction of labor (1975:162), and function as a basic form of gift exchange (1975:173), among others.

8    Gayatri C. Spivak borrows the term "subaltern" from Antonio Gramsci, for whom the subaltern was the repressed peasant, and suggests that it is an intellectually and politically loaded term, functionally oppositional to "dominant" or "elite" (1988:1). As regards the subaltern woman, Spivak suggests that she is a figure that moves from clan to clan as "daughter/sister and wife/mother [and who] syntaxes patriarchal continuity even as she is herself drained of proper identity" (1988:31). Thus, her consciousness cannot be fully recovered (1988:12) because its interpreters are always subject to the ideology of the elite and it is always "askew from its received signifiers ... it is effaced even as it is disclosed" (1988:11). Indeed, such a woman "disappears" into what Spivak calls "a violent aporia between subject and object status" (1988:306). Since, she argues, the subaltern male cannot express himself in terms that are understood by the imperialist, then the subaltern female is "even more deeply in shadow" (1988: 287) and is mute. In addition, the very terms of her existence are dictated to her by the oppressor and this implicates her in her own oppression.

9    Many postcolonial novels are concerned with visions of alternate worlds characterized by freedom and equality, faith, and security. These alternate or possible worlds are made real in the minds of the postcolonial subjects by a kind of internalization of concepts of race, class, and gender that are at odds with the neo-colonial world that surrounds them. Thus, the subjects create alternative histories and identities for themselves that set

them apart from their environment. Some novels that conceptualize alternate worlds are: Tsitsi Dangaremba's *Nervous Conditions*, Bessie Head's *A Question of Power*, Nadine Gordimer's *Burger's Daughter*, Nayantara Sahgal's *This Time of Morning*, Doris Lessing's *Four Gated City*, and Gabriel Garcia-Marquez's *One Hundred Years of Solitude*.

## WORKS CITED

Althusser, Louis. 1990. *For Marx.* Trans. Ben Brewster. London and New York: Verso.

Amuta, Chidi. 1984. "History, Society and Heroism in the Nigerian War Novel." *Kunapipi* 6 (3): 57-70.

Barrett, Michele. 1980. *Women's Oppression Today: Problems in Marxist Feminist Analysis.* London: Verso.

Barthelemy, Anthony. 1989. "Western Time, African Lives: Time in the Novels of Buchi Emecheta." *Callaloo: A Journal of Afro-American and African Arts and Letters* 12 (3): 559-574.

Brown, Lloyd W. 1981. "Buchi Emecheta," in his *Women Writers in Black Africa.* Contributions in Women's Studies 21. Westport and London: Greenwood Press :35- 60.

Emecheta, Buchi. 1976. *The Bride Price.* London: Allison and Busby; New York: Braziller.

_____. *Destination Biafra.* 1982. London and New York: Allison and Busby.

_____. *Double Yoke.* 1983. New York: Braziller. First published in Umuezeokda and London: 1982.

_____. *Second Class Citizen.* 1975. New York: Braziller. First published in London: 1974.

Emenyonu, Ernest N. 1988. "Technique and Language in Buchi Emecheta's *The Bride Price, The Slave Girl,* and *The Joys of Motherhood. The Journal of Commonwealth Literature* 23 (1): 130-141.

Frank, Katherine. 1982. "The Death of the Slave Girl: African Womanhood in the Novels of Buchi Emecheta." *World Literature Written in English* 21 (3): 476-497.

Gates, Henry Louis, Jr. 1985 and 1986. "Writing 'Race' and the Difference It Makes." Introduction to "Race, Writing and Difference." *Critical Inquiry*

12 (1): 1-19. Rpt. in: Henry Louis Gates, Jr. ed. *"Race," Writing and Difference.* Chicago and London: University of Chicago Press: 1-20.

Irigaray, Luce. 1985. *Speculum of the Other Woman.* Trans. Gillian C. Gill. Ithaca: Cornell University Press. First published in French: 1974.

Jameson, Fredric. 1981. *The Political Unconscious: Narrative as a Socially Symbolic Act.* Ithaca: Cornell University Press.

Katrak, Ketu. 1987. "Womanhood/Motherhood: Variations on a Theme in Selected Novels of Buchi Emecheta." *Journal of Commonwealth Literature* 22 (1): 159-170.

Lerner, Gerda. 1986. *The Creation of Patriarchy.* Women and History 1. New York and Oxford: Oxford University Press.

Macherey, Pierre. 1978. *A Theory of Literary Production.* Trans. Geoffrey Wall. London and New York: Routledge. First published in French: 1966.

Mishra, Vijay and Bob Hodge. 1994. "What is Post(-)colonialism?" In Williams and Chrisman: 276-290.

Simpson, J. A. and E.S.C. Weiner (preparers). 1989. *The Oxford English Dictionary.* 2nd edition. 20 volumes. Oxford: Clarendon; Oxford and New York: Oxford University Press.

Rubin, Gayle. 1975. "The Traffic in Women: Notes on the 'Political Economy' of Sex." In *Towards an Anthropology of Women.* Rayna R. Reiter, Ed. New York: Monthly Review Press.

Sangari, Kumkum and Sudesh Vaid (eds.). 1990. *Recasting Women: Essays in Indian Colonial History.* New Brunswick: Rutgers University Press.

Solberg, Rolf. 1983. "The Woman of Black Africa, Buchi Emecheta: The Woman's Voice in the New Nigerian Novel." *English Studies: A Journal of English Language and Literature* 64 (3): 247-261.

Spivak, Gayatri Chakravorty. 1988. "Can the Subaltern Speak?" In *Marxism and the Interpretation of Culture.* Cary Nelson and Lawrence Grossberg, Ed. Urbana: University of Illinois Press: 271-313.

_____. 1988. "Subaltern Studies: Deconstructing Historiography." In *Selected Subaltern Studies*. Ranajit Guha and Gayatri Chakravorty Spivak, Ed. New York and Oxford: Oxford University Press: 3-32.

Taiwo, Oladele. 1984. "Buchi Emecheta," in her *Female Novelists of Modern Africa*. London: Macmillan: 100-127.

Ward, Cynthia. 1990. "What They Told Buchi Emecheta: Oral Subjectivity and the Joys of 'Otherhood'." *Publications of the Modern Language Association of America* 105 (1): 83-97.

Williams, Patrick and Laura Chrisman (eds.). 1994. *Colonial Discourse and Post-Colonial Theory: A Reader*.   New York: Columbia University Press.

Wren, Robert M. 1980. *Achebe's World: The Historical and Cultural Context of the Novels*. Washington, D.C.: Three Continents Press.

# CHAPTER TEN

**Flora Nwapa's Final Legacy: Dramatic Elements in *The Sychophants***

**Ernest N. Emenyonu**

When Flora Nwapa died on October 16, 1993, the literary world mourned the passing of a historic pioneer, Africa's first female Black novelist. African feminists mourned the passing of a mother-figure who, in 1966, gave female writers in Africa a confident tongue and an authentic pen with her novel, *Efuru*. The publishing industry in Africa mourned the loss of a pace-setter entrepreneur whose Tana Press established in 1976 in Enugu, Nigeria, was the first modern publishing company in Black Africa to be singly and totally owned by a woman. Eastern Nigeria had lost the first woman to be appointed to an important substantive cabinet position in the government, for two decades earlier, Flora Nwapa had been the Minister in charge first, of Social Welfare and Youth Development, and later, Lands and Urban Development. The litany of "firsts" in Flora Nwapa's life and career stretches from achievements in creative writing to cultural recognitions in the award of chieftaincy titles. She was an acknowledged successful novelist, an engaging short story writer at home with both the rural and urban environments. She had established herself as a serious poet with the publication of her *Cassava Song and Rice Song* in 1986. She had also gained favorable reputation as author of children's stories with *Emeka, The Driver's Guard* (1972) and *Mammy Water* (1979) as her most popular titles.

Flora Nwapa, however, had other literary talents of which the most hidden until her death, was her accomplishment as a versatile playwright. In the year that she died, she wrote three full length plays, two of which are devastatingly provocative in themes, and the third, a landmark in its ebullient satire on Nigeria's social, economic and political systems. The plays, *The First Lady, Two Women in Conversation,* and *The Sychophants* were all published in 1993 in the week that Flora Nwapa died from complications in arthritis and pneumonia at the University of Nigeria Teaching Hospital, Enugu. Unfortunately these highly explosive and socially relevant plays are yet to reach the literary world thirsting for them, as only about ten copies of each were produced for Flora Nwapa's solace on her deathbed. Since the death of its founder, Tana Press (which produced the few copies of the plays) has remained in a comatose of sorts. Unless and until an enterprising publisher steps in, the literary world may be denied these rare gems for many more years to come. If Flora Nwapa had lived, her reputation as a playwright probably might have enhanced or surpassed her image as a novelist. Most certainly her dialectical ambivalence towards feminism as a movement would have been a thing of the past, for in *The First Lady* and *Two Women in Conversation* her identification with feminism in Africa and elsewhere is pragmatically and ideologically total.

In all three plays Nwapa displays the most effusive militancy in her denunciation of all forms of social injustice, gender inequities and corrupt politics in her society. It was as if she had given up on Nigeria and had used these plays to wreak seeming vengeance on all those who, through their corrupt practices and aberrant leadership, turned the Nigerian society from gold into dust. The mood is unrelentingly pessimistic. In *The First Lady* the focus is on lack of political direction which has brought about a breakdown in law and order and the deterioration of the quality of life and human condition. We have such undisguised authorial intrusions as:

> What a country! No regular water supply, no
> electricity and no telephone facility ... (60)
> ... Everybody is a law unto himself ... (111)
> ... This is Nigeria. Anything can happen here ... The
> false can become the true and the true false (119)
> ... I have lost faith in democracy and the ballot box

... No wonder the soldiers keep coming back ... we
have destroyed our country ... We paid in 1966.
Then we fought the civil war. We have shed blood...
But we shall pay again ... We are not ready yet for
the rule of law and democracy. *(173/4)*

In *Two Women in Conversation,* the vehemence is on assaults on women
(including domestic violence), and the dehumanization of womanhood by abusive
patriarchy and feudalistic tradition. Marriage as a modern social institution is
similarly wished out of existence. "As I see it, the institution of marriage will
soon disappear from the face of the earth" (122). In this, the most poignant of the
three plays, the two women (whose subject of conversation is tyranny in
marriage) alternate at critical points in the conversation as Nwapa's apparent alter
ego in their acid utterances about errant husbands and abusive men.

In the third play, *The Sychophants* which is the focus of this study, Nwapa
unexpectedly diverts attention from womanhood and feminine concerns to the
mundane destruction of Nigerian youth by insipid bureaucracy, endemic
corruption and acrimonious politics. The picture is one of a country that
consciously or unconsciously destroys its youthful citizenry through
unemployment, mental torture and spiritual stagnation leaving thereby, its
posterity without a future of hope. What is most striking about this play is
Nwapa's effortless use of piercing satire and sardonic irony; artistic elements
which have never before been experienced to this scale in Nwapa's fiction.

Unlike *The First Lady* which has a vast array of characters mostly women,
and *Two Women in Conversation* where the protagonists are female with male
presence felt only in shadows, *The Sychophants* has two male protagonists and
there are no implicit or explicit gender conflicts in the play. The play is set in
Lagos, the erstwhile capital city of Nigeria, where the two men Miki and Poki
now in their forties, have lived all their lives and can recall no affinity whatsoever
with their village roots. Nwapa casts them as "Lost" socially, culturally, mentally,
and spiritually. They have become the "wretched" of their society and represent

thousands or millions of other disenfranchised, exploited, marginalized or unemployed citizenry who have no visions of tomorrow but dream dreams of instant wealth through shady contracts from the government. They reflect the inertia and total lack of direction in both the ruled and the rulers in the country.

> We are
> What we are,
> Sychophants.
> We are doomed
> To sing the praises
> Of the government
> Of the day.
> It is not our business
> To criticize the policies
> Of Government
> For we know
> That these policies
> Were reached
> After long and grave
> Deliberations
> By experts and knowledgeable
> Women and men,
> Whether they be military
> Men in khaki
> Or civilians in *agbada*. *(35-6)*

When the play opens Miki and Poki are discussing two recent government edicts aimed at curbing unemployment and ridding the city of ubiquitous undesirable elements. The first decree "abolished street trading" and the second decree commanded those concerned to "Go to the Farm." The concerned citizens are the destitute, the poor, the beggars and the homeless who find shelter in:

> Bus stops
> Under the bridges
> Market places. (9)

Nwapa identifies them in capital letters as "THEY, THEM, THEIRS" and their language with its admixture of slangs and vernacular expressions identifies their class. They have defied the decrees and are everywhere in Lagos causing discomfort to travelers and the elite. The street hawkers among them are "desperate, aggressive and hawk everything under the sun," disrupting traffic and creating irritating inconveniences. The government decrees characteristically have no visible practical *modus operandi* for enforcement. The sychophants Miki and Poki offer to help the government enforce the decrees. They believe that the government had made a fundamental error in judgment:

> Why make a law
> When you know
> That its enforcement
> Is near impossible?
> ... The cause of street trading
> Is unemployment
> Pure and simple.
> So what Government
> Should have done
> Was to abolish
> Unemployment.
> ... Give jobs to everybody
> To all the hawkers
> On the streets of Lagos
> Then if you see THEM
> Back on the streets
> Arrest THEM (7)

Since Government was not insightful enough to do this, Miki and Poki have a grand design to help the government; a grand design through which the playwright caricatures and lampoons the government and its executives.

The grand design is to build forty-two youth camps not just for Lagos but for all the capital and major cities throughout the country. The youth camps will cost a total of 210 million naira at five million each. The camps will put these undesirable elements out of sight and offer them the opportunity to now farm. Miki and Poki will sell this pragmatic idea to the government and persuade the government to award them the contract to build the camps, except that following the common practice in the country and the examples of the government officials, they have no real intention to build anything.

> Our concern is not
> To see the camps built.
> ... Our main concern
> Is to see that the contract
> Is awarded to us.
> ... When the contract paper
> Is in our hands
> We sell it.
> Finish!
> ... Finito!
> ... Opari!! (68-9)

Within this framework Flora Nwapa weaves her wide net of social criticisms where various public institutions, utilities and government agencies, military and civilian regimes, and the entire political and economic systems in the country are caricatured, ridiculed and lampooned. The government, whether military or civilian, is x-rayed in the open through the attitudes and performances of both its executives and public institutions. Each unit is exposed in its full ramifications, but in general, "what makes me sad, is that the greatest problem in our country today,"...

> ... is not so much
> Bribery and corruption.
> It is waste -
> Waste of human resources
> Waste of manpower
> Waste of food
> Waste of time and energy
> Doing the wrong things;
> Waste of words
> Waste of money
> In the name of grandeur;
> Waste of titles
> Given to the wrong people... (27)

This is a sad and sordid picture of political decadence, social decay and general atrophy, but the playwright admonishes through her character Poki that, "You gotta laugh to cry" because:

> You have to have a sense of humour
> To be in this business
> And live in Nigeria
> Otherwise, you will commit murder.
> Humour is better. You can keep
> Your sanity with humour. (42)

Humor is necessary when you encounter top government officials who give people important appointments in their offices when they know they would be away in Hong Kong, and their secretaries will have you wait when you show up for the appointment.

> You should not complain
> You live in Lagos.
> What about those
> Who travel all the way
> From Sokoto or Maiduguri
> To see the BIG MAN in Lagos
> On appointment, mind you
> On appointment
> Only to be told on arrival that
> The BIG MAN
> Had gone to Timbuktu? (43)

Humor is needed when you encounter a Military Governor (in a corrective regime) in total ecstasy on receiving a bribe from an unknown civilian citizen. We see the governor clearly through excellent and detailed stage directions:

> As CHIEF SAPA exists (exits?) the GOVERNOR
> returns to his seat. He then sees the briefcase which
> CHIEF SAPA has apparently forgotten. He is
> initially suspicious. He picks up his telephone, dials
> a number, thinks, and drops the receiver. He picks
> up the brief case and looks at it, admiringly. He sees
> the inscription on the brief case and starts. He reads
> his name aloud, showing signs of confusion. He
> tries to weigh the brief case in his hands. It shows
> evidence of weight. He then proceeds to open the
> leather brief case with his two fore-fingers. He
> presses the gold locks. The brief case automatically
> opens .

> My goodness!
> What do we have here?
> Money!
>
> The GOVERNOR goes back to the notes and begins
> to caress them with enthusiasm. He picks some and
> kisses them, looking frantically at the door to ensure
> that nobody is eavesdropping on him. (48-9)

The irony is not lost on the audience because of an earlier established background knowledge:

> When the new military rulers
> Firmly established themselves (after a Coup!)
> Promising heaven and earth
> How justice would prevail,
> How corruption would be
> Wiped out from the face
> Of the earth... (23)

Irony is a strong weapon in the major conflicts in the play. The corrective military regime had inherited from the toppled civilian government a completed but unequipped hospital built for a large section of the population in a rural area. The military governor cold not equip the hospital because he was confused by an avalanche of conflicting petitions which claimed either that the land on which the hospital was built was in dispute, or that the land was formerly a shrine of the gods (and instead of equipping the hospital, he should be appeasing the gods) or still, the people needed a market (not a hospital) "to stem the tide of our young women marrying from neighbouring villages." In spite of "the knowledgeable experts" who advise the governor, the "Poor Military Governor" in the end,

> .... was so confused
> He ended up doing nothing. (27)

Nwapa shows mockingly how a government, in a military regime for that matter, could allow itself to be manipulated, diverted, cajoled, fooled and rendered totally irrelevant by mere anonymous petitions. Everything, everyone moves in circles and nothing serious or important gets done even at the highest level of government.

This mental debility in the rulers is responsible for their nonchalant attitude towards institutions of higher learning which have been reduced to mockery and insignificance in the national scheme of things:

> You are laughing
> Because the age
> Of the Ivory Tower
> Is gone and gone forever. (54)

The university students cannot be "distinguished from the rest of the mob." Nwapa introduces into the play familiar cliches and slangs by which Nigerian undergraduates express the deplorable social and environmental decay on the university campuses. "Zero-one-zero," "Zero-zero-one", "One-zero-zero" describe the feeding patterns of students since the government's abolition of catering services in all the universities. "Zero" stands for any of the three meals (breakfast, lunch, dinner) which the students, because of their poor economic conditions, cannot afford. The devastating irony in the situation is that the undergraduate students (the so-called leaders of tomorrow) have been reduced to a situation where the sychophants see them as worse and lower in esteem than the dregs of society for whom they are proposing the youth camps.

> The people in the camps
> Which we are going to build
> Will have three square meals
> Aday. (55)

They conclude that not having an education in the Nigerian society is no longer a handicap because,

> Going to school
> Used to be a big deal
> Not any more.
> University graduates now

> Roam the streets of Lagos
> In search of jobs
> They know are not there. (66)

Like other government policies enunciated by "knowledgeable experts," the new government policy on catering in the universities has resulted in starving the students, while the policy severely restricting accommodation and boarding facilities has resulted in "ten students sleeping in rooms meant for two" with unimaginable health consequences. The so-called government experts have anything but expertise. The opposite is the truth. The policies in practice suggest thoughtless, irrational, flash-in-the-pan schemes which only add to the social quagmire and national predicament.

If the message and moral preoccupations in *The Sychophants* are so succinctly portrayed, Nwapa's literary and dramatic techniques in the play are even more remarkable. Nigerian slogans and linguistic expressions unique to Nigerian English, occur frequently in the play to reinforce the setting and establish the target audience. They are in places juxtaposed with vernacular words which Nwapa does not attempt to interpret or explain, leaving the reader of the play to deduce the meanings from the context. Thus we have expressions such as "okpari, omasie-o, Omo Eko, kee, agbada" (Yoruba), buka, Dogon Turenchi (Hausa). The comic expression "plus and including" (12) is drawn from a popular Nigerian TV situation comedy, "The Masquerades" where the inimitable hero Zebrudaya coins new words and English expressions at random and with reckless abandon. The expression "the lady throws away her face" (39) is a unique Nigerian usage which means that the lady ignored whoever was trying to draw her attention by gesture or verbal communication, while "for where?" (42) is used to emphasize a situation where something was expected to happen but never did.

Explicit stage directions are used to establish appropriate settings and convey effectively nonverbal communications such as miming, body movements and gestures and unique physical or verbal mannerisms which cannot otherwise be authentically depicted. Lighting is used to great technical effect in establishing sequences and dramatic realism. The lights alternate from fading, to clear, to dark which symbolically convey distinguishing moods and draw attention to differences between substance and shadow, viable and unviable actions and schemes. Flashbacks are used to achieve continuity in plot and proper sequence of events and actions.

Nwapa also uses such technical devices as capitalization of words and names to suggest emphasis on caricature. The low class is identified as 'THEY, THESE, THEM" and the capitalization establishes the class differences and the social attitudes towards them. They are underprivileged and are treated as such by the government and the elite. They are outcasts and don't belong even though they have grown in numbers and scope to include unemployed undergraduates.

Nwapa's chosen title, "The Sychophants" has symbolic connotations. The manifested imbecility of the duo, Miki and Poki, their in-trance-like mentality (as well as that of the few lesser characters), most evident when they build their castles in the air, is a reflection of the larger society where nothing is planned properly; things happen on impulse, events move rapidly like twinkling shadows and effigies suggesting lack of proper rational thought. They also reflect the mood of the nation. It is a mood of empty euphoric ecstasy in the process of which frivolous ideas are mistaken as grandiose national development plans.

Flora Nwapa has said quite succinctly in a sixty-nine page play what could not have been deciphered from a voluminous novel or from hundreds of massive official reports. She knows her Nigerian people and environments very well and depicts them with flawless authenticity. She brings into these depictions a sense of humor which mocks as it entertains and elicits laughter. One should not grieve over the looting of national treasury as "the money is not yours, it is not your father's either; it is *only* Government money" (22). The use of the word *only* emphasizes the trivial nature of the unnecessary concern. Bribery has a network and a traffic. It is not a moral issue; what it demands and tests are your ability and astuteness "to know somebody, Who knows somebody there." The connection could be as spurious and contrived as ever, but that does not matter; all is legitimate:

> I know somebody
> Whose sister
> Is related to the brother
> Of the friend of
> The Minister of Works... (60)

Nwapa has sharp eyes and alert ears for accurate details of civil servants' mannerisms, the inertia of government executives, the frivolity of government advisers and the digressing gossips of secretaries in government offices, and she records these with flawless authenticity. The social degradation is at its lowest ebb when "the difference between a Chief and a Thief", is that:

> One is the custodian
> Of our culture
> By day,
> The other is the custodian
> Of our culture
> By night... (64)

Flora Nwapa, after experimenting with the novel, the short story, and poetry to reform the social malaise in her society, must have resorted as a last option to drama in which she sought to speak plainly and directly to Nigerians and their leaders in a language they could both clearly understand. *The Sychophants* has a pessimistic tone and ending, but it has a powerful message which no one familiar with the Nigerian political landscape of the last three decades can miss. The playwright has "lost faith in the ballot box" (Nigerian style) and believes that "Nigerians are not yet ready for the rule of law and democracy." That notwithstanding, the solution will not be found,

> Through the barrel
> Of a gun.
> Nor through a revolution.
> Revolution is not the answer,

>Violent revolution,
>Shedding of blood
>Is not the answer.
>If we seek change
>For the good of our country
>We should start from within. (31)

The successful transformation of Nigerians from "shady contractors to true patriots," which is Nwapa's grand political message in *The Sychophants* depends,

>On the entire Nigerian people.
>Change, I think,
>Will come from within
>Not from without
>Nigeria will be great
>ffyouandl
>Realise that we have a part
>To play
>In bringing about this change. (30)

## WORKS CITED

Flora Nwapa, *Two Women in Conversation*, Enugu, Nigeria, Tana Press, 1993.

_____. *The First Lady*, Enugu, Nigeria, Tana Press, 1993

_____. *The Sychophants*, Enugu, Nigeria, Tana Press, 1993.

# CHAPTER ELEVEN

**Grace Nichols'** *I is a Long Memoried Woman*
**and Julie Dash's** *Daughters of the Dust*: **Reversing the Middle Passage**
**Jacquelyn Benton**


In their analyses of Black literature, some critics have brought together works by African and Diasporic peoples in order to establish cross-cultural linkages. This trend has been particularly noticeable in the works of Black female critics who have posited that the experiences of Black women worldwide consist of common elements. One such critic is Abena Busia. In her essay, "Words Whispered over Voids: A Context for Black Women's Rebellious Voices in the Novel of the African Diaspora," she asks:

> Does an urban, Senegalese Muslim woman writing after the experience of twentieth-century French colonial rule truly have anything in common with the descendants of former slaves living out their lives as poor black Christians in the rural American South? And if not, is it really sufficient to make a case for unity simply because both happen to be both black and female? For us, the answer must, unequivocably, be yes. (2)

Busia goes on to examine works by African, African-American, and Caribbean women, arguing that these women write from the common space of racial and sexual marginalization, and as such, common themes surface in their works.

Busia's point is well taken; however, one theme also sets African and Diasporic women apart. Whether physical or metaphorical, the "return to Africa" continues to be of particular concern to Diasporic women writers. This concern is apparent in *I is a Long Memoried Woman*, a book length poem by Caribbean-born Grace Nichols, and *Daughters of the Dust*, the first feature film of African-American Julie Dash. In both works the journey back is accomplished through the overlapping themes of resistance and memory.

*I is a Long Memoried Woman* has been described as "a kind of psychic history of the whole of Caribbean womanhood" ("Grace" 18). The book was inspired by a dream Nichols had of a young girl swimming from Africa to the Caribbean with a garland of flowers. Nichols stated, "When I woke up I interpreted the dream to mean that she was trying to cleanse the ocean of the pain and suffering that she knew her ancestors had gone through" (18). A slim volume of fifty-one poems, *I is a Long Memoried Woman* can be seen as one book-length poem divided into five sections, each section signaling a different stage in the journey of an unnamed woman. The first poem begins on board a slave ship as the story of the "child of the Middle Passage womb" begins to unfold. The description of her passage reveals that the entire book will be related as a memory:

> she came
> into the new world
> birth aching her pain
> from one continent/to another
> .....
> and after fifty years
> she hasn't forgotten
> hasn't forgotten
> how she had lain there
> in her own blood lain there
> in her own shit
>
> bleeding memories in the darkness (Nichols 6)

The repetition of "hasn't forgotten" indicates that this was not a journey that *could* be forgotten and substantiates its lingering presence in the literature.

*Daughters of the Dust* also relates a journey. Ostensibly, it is the story of the Peazants, a family living in the Sea Islands of the South in the United States.

The Peazants are members of a Gullah community, people who during slavery were able to maintain much of their African culture because of their isolation from the mainland. Set in 1902, the film opens as younger family members are preparing to leave the islands and move to cities in the northern United States. They will leave behind Nana Peazant, the family matriarch, who wants to ensure that they leave the island with a strong sense of self. She says to them, "Never forget who we are and how far we've come' (Dash 96). A former slave, Nana is alluding to that slave past, as well as the unknown African past. The film's story, however, is actually the journey taken by African-Americans from slavery through the Great Migration.

Slavery assumes the focus in both works, Nichols' poem chronicling the slave experience in the Caribbean and Dash's film emphasizing the legacies of slavery in the United States. Women occupy the centers of both works, the slave experience being recalled through female eyes. Both too address ways in which women responded to their oppression, and it is here that the book and the film overlap at the sites of resistance and memory. It is also here that the "return to Africa" is made clear.

In literature and film, resistance to slavery has generally been articulated in terms of slave uprisings and other incidents of physical altercation. Resonances of this are present in *I is a Long Memoried Woman* when the spirits of Toussaint L'Ouverture, the Haitian leader, and Nanny, the Jamaican National Heroine, are evoked near the end of the text. Under Toussaint's leadership, the slaves were able to drive the French out of Haiti and claim their freedom, and Nanny, the legendary military leader, led the Maroons to victory against the British. However, women's resistance generally follows a different course, the example of Nanny notwithstanding. And it is the other forms that resistance can take that achieve prominence in the text. In the poem "Waterpot," for example, the narrative voice relates the daily comings and goings to and from the cane fields where the slaves are always hurried along "like...like cattle" (Nichols 14). And yet:

> In the evenings
> returning from the fields
> she tried hard to walk
> like a woman
>
> she tried very hard
> pulling herself erect
> with every three or four
> steps
> pulling herself like
> royal cane (14)

Here resistance is displayed in the desire to walk "like a woman," even though treated like cattle. The woman's identification with sugar cane acknowledges her oppression, yet she does not allow her circumstances to make her forget who she is. Acknowledgement of that, however, is at a cost. Her proud bearing is borne only through effort, since it must be *consciously* resumed "with every three or four steps." And she endures the overseer's sneer at what he perceives as "the pathetic-the pathetic display/of dignity" (14), but this is no deterrent for the true dignity that she reveals. However, resistance in "Ala" takes a different shape. This poem opens with the following lines:

> Face up
> they hold her naked body
> to the ground
> arms and legs spread-eagle
> each tie with rope to stake
>
> then they coat her in sweet
> molasses and call us out
> to see ..... the rebel woman (Nichols 23)

The rebel woman's act is reminiscent of that of Sethe, the protagonist of Toni Morrison's Pulitzer Prize winning novel *Beloved*, who wanted freedom for her children. Morrison created this character after reading the newspaper account of Margaret Garner, an actual slave in the United States, who chose death for her child over a life of slavery. This was not an uncommon act during slavery. In her book, *Natural Rebels: A Social History of Enslaved Black Women in Barbados*, Hilary Beckles states, "There is yet no concrete evidence that slave women practiced what has become known as 'gynaecological resistance.' although planters believed that the birth control techniques used were an attempt to reduce the flow of labour to the estates. But acts of infanticide are frequently cited in plantation records" (159).

In the poem, the coated body of the rebel woman is left at the mercy of red ants and the sun. And it is here that sticking the pin in "her own child's head" carries a certain irony. For the harsh punishment the woman receives is not motivated by her killing *her own child.* Since the child would have been considered the slave-owner's property, it is the property loss which provides the motivation for the punishment. In Margaret Garner's case-as Toni Morrison has explained-the crime Garner was tried for was stolen property ("Writer's), since she escaped slavery taking her children with her. The rebel woman then resists on two levels: she refuses to add to the property of the slave-owner, and she does, in fact, claim her child, since she determines its fate.

One section of poems explores sorcery as a means of resistance. In "Night is Her Robe," a woman goes into the forest and "with all the care/of a herbalist" gathers weeds, roots, and "leaves with the property/both to harm and to heal" (Nichols 47). In "Old Magic," a woman identifies herself as "the mirror/you break in seven pieces/the curse you think/you leave behind...the one you going/sleep with/the one you going/think is kind" (48). These poems are leading up to "Love Act," where the woman is summoned to the slave-owner's home:

> She enter his Great House
> her see-far looking eyes
> unassuming
>
> .....
> He want to tower above her
> want her to raise her ebony
> haunches and when she does
> he thinks she can be trusted

and drinks her in (49)

The title of this poem is ironic, "love" being no descriptor of this act, and the word "act" itself taking on a dual meaning. The act the woman will put on is indicated by "her see-far looking eyes/unassuming," and ultimately the facade will allow her to entrap the slave-owner and his family. At the end of the poem:

> Her sorcery cut them
> like a whip
>
> She hide her triumph
> and slowly stir the hate
> of poison in (49)

Although different, all these acts of resistance have a common element. The woman who resists with her proud bearing is resuming the posture of her African upbringing, for "...look/there's a waterpot growing/from her head" (Nichols 14); the woman who kills her child sent "...the little-new-born/soul winging its way back/to Africa-free" (23; and the woman in the poems dealing with sorcery is using knowledge brought with her from Africa. Grounded in recall of the African past, these acts acknowledge the role that memory plays in resistance, a role central to *Daughters of the Dust*.

Though almost fifty years removed from the period of slavery in the United States, the Peazant family must still reckon with the sexual exploitation apparent in Nichols' poem "Love Act." Yellow Mary Peazant has returned to the islands from Cuba, where her employers took her to serve as a wet nurse for their child. Though the scenes in Cuba were omitted from the film, Yellow Mary is forced to submit to the child's father and succeeds in getting away from the family only by drying up her breast milk. She says, "I wanted to go home and they keep me. ..they keep me....So I 'fix' the titty...they send me home" (Dash 126). Toni Cade Bambara likens Yellow Mary's act to that of a "factory worker on strike" (126). Yet one could also say that she is practicing the "gynaecological resistance" that Hilary Beckles was reluctant to acknowledge.

However, the issue of sexual exploitation focuses most directly on Eula Peazant, who at the outset of the film has been raped by a wealthy landowner. Now pregnant, Eula must deal with her husband's fear that the child she carries is not his. Her resistance to her circumstances comes in the form of retelling the story of Ibo Landing.

In the film, Ibo Landing is the site on the Sea Islands where African slaves first arrived into the New World. However, upon arrival they foresaw the fate that awaited them and chose not to stay. Instead, they walked back into the water and continued on home to Africa. Eula says:

> Now you wouldn't think they'd get very far seeing
> as it was water they was walking on. They had all
> that iron upon them. Upon their ankles and their
> wrists, and fastened around their necks like dog
> collars. But chains didn't stop those Ibo. They just
> kept walking, like the water was solid ground.
> (Dash 142)

The wording of the tale is taken from *Praisesong for the Widow*, a novel by African-American Paule Marshall; however, the story itself is part of Sea Island history. Dash says, "[I]n my research, I found that almost every Sea Island has a little inlet, or a little area where the people say, 'This is Ibo Landing. This is where it happened...'" (Dialogue 30). Dash goes on to say that many Gullah communities claim this story because its message is "so strong, so powerful, so sustaining to the tradition of resistance, by any means possible" (30). Bilal Muhammed, a character in the film, says that instead of walking, the Ibo "flew back home to Africa" (Dash 152). His statement links the tale to the Flying African motif, a motif that resonates throughout the African-American storytelling tradition.

In a children's book entitled, *Imani and the Flying Africans*, a young boy hears a story told to him by his mother of slaves who flew back to Africa to escape captivity. In *The Book of Negro Folklore*, the story "All God's Chillen Had Wings" tells the story of slaves who remembering "what they had forgotten, and...the power which once had been theirs" took flight and returned to Africa (Hughes 64). Another book, *The People Could Fly*, contains a short story of the same title, which is a variation of the previous story. The flying motif also enters into *Song of Solomon*, Toni Morrison's third novel, when the character Milkman takes to the air in a reenactment of the flight of his ancestor Solomon, one of the Flying Africans (341).

In *Daughters of the Dust*, it is significant that the story of Ibo Landing is given to Eula to tell. She must deal with the ordeal of the rape she has endured, as well as keep her attacker's identity a secret in order to protect her husband Eli. As Yellow Mary tells her, "He [Eli] doesn't need to know what could get him killed.... There's enough uncertainty in life without having to sit at home wondering which tree your husband's hanging from....Don't tell him nothing" (Dash 123-4). Yellow Mary is alluding to the lynching of Black men prevalent during this time period. Since Eula is powerless to resist her circumstances in any overt way, one could say that she is simply drawing comfort from the story of those who were able to cast off their oppression; however, the importance of the tale lies as much in its retelling as in the tale itself.

As Eula narrates the story, both of her hands are holding her stomach. She is passing down the tale to her unborn child, a tale passed down to her by her grandmother. "Well, they saw just about everything that was to happen around here... The slavery time, the war my grandmother always talks about...Those Ibo didn't miss a thing. They even saw you and I standing here talking" (141), she tells her child. Eula's retelling of the story links her and her child to the Africans whose story she tells. And in doing so, the tale is activated-as her husband Eli demonstrates.

Eli's distress over his wife's rape has been expressed in terms of ownership. At one point, he says to Nana Peazant, "This happened to my wife. My wife! I don't feel like she's mine anymore. When I look at her, I feel I don't want her anymore" (Dash 95). And later he speaks of Eula having been "ridden" by a stranger. African-American critic Bell Hooks says of his remarks:

> One effect of Eli saying, 'My wife, and some other man was riding her' is that it allows us to see that there is a connection between his own phallocentricity, his patriarchal sense of ownership, and the mentality of the unknown rapist.. ..It is Nana Peazant who has to come in and remind him that...he has another tradition that he can relate to and which can give him a sense of masculinity that is not disrupted by the actions of the oppressor ("Dialogue" 50).

Nana's response to Eli, to which hooks alludes, was "You can't give back what you never owned. Eula never belonged to you, she married you" (Dash 95).

Nana has also beseeched Eli to "[c]all on those old Africans." She says, "Let them fill your head with wisdom that ain't from this day and time" (97). It is an intervention from the ancestors that allows Eli to heed her words. "Ridden" in a true sense, he walks out onto the waters of Ibo Landing as his wife narrates the tale. And like Milkman in *Song of Solomon*, who reenacted the flight of his flying ancestor, so too Eli feels the water hold him up. A note in the film's screenplay says, "Under the whip and guidance of his ancestral spirit-rider, Eli has witnessed and performed things that he could not have done "unridden" (Dash 142). Resolution for Eula and Eli lay in cultural memory, the story of Ibo Landing narrating resistance, but more important, *functioning* as resistance.

Memory and resistance intersect not only in content of *Daughters of the Dust* and *I is a Long Memoried Woman* but also in form, since both Nichols and Dash have chosen to ground their works in the African oral tradition. In her essay on 'Writing the Body,' Gabriele Griffin describes Nichols' work as "aligned to an oral tradition which takes its rhythms and inflections from the body. Breaks are created not by punctuation but by the need to draw breath, by how the body moves as it recites..." (26). Griffin is choosing to emphasize "the body" in her piece, but her words speak to the performative nature of the oral tale, which Nichols seeks to recreate. And film critic Ed Guerrero says that Julie Dash relied on a "cultural heirloom, the African oral tradition shaded with the narrative sensibilities of the griot" (176) in order to tell her story.

In constructing their stories by recalling an African art form, Nichols and Dash are at the same time resisting Western models. Nichols has said that she wanted something that sounded and looked different "to the eye on the page and to the ear," something in contrast to the English poetry she had read (Griffin 32), and Dash was part of the L.A. Rebellion, a group of Black filmmakers who sought to create a new film language which contrasted with classical Hollywood cinema. Dash also chose to pattern her characters after deity from the Yoruba mythology, rather than using Western archetypes. So Eli Peazant, for example, is patterned after Ogun and Yellow Mary Peazant after Yemoja, deity that Nichols also makes use of in *I is a Long Memoried Woman.*

In harkening back to the African past through the form and content of their works, Grace Nichols and Julie Dash reveal that they themselves are long memoried women, their works attesting to the value that they place on "remembering." Like Nana Peazant, they are saying, "Never forget who we are, and how far we've come." And the importance of memory and reconnection which they claim signals their reversal of the Middle Passage.

In Nichols' dream of the African girl swimming to the Caribbean, the young girl was addressing the pain of the ancestors; Nichols and Dash are addressing the pain of the descendants, indicating that healing for an oppressed people often lies in remembering. Yes, the recurring return to Africa theme in the works of Diasporic women writers does separate them from their African sisters. But then again, it brings them together.

## WORKS CITED

"All God's Chillen Had Wings." 1959. Story by Caesar Grant of John's Island. In *The Book of Negro Folklore*, pp.62-65. Edited by Langston Hughes and Ama Bontemps. New York: Dodd.

Baker, Jr., Houston A. 1992. "Not Without My *Daughters*. A conversation with Julie Dash and Houston A. Baker, Jr." *Transition* 57 November 1992: 151-166.

Bambara, Toni Cade. 1993. "Reading the Signs, Empowering the Eye: *Daughters of the Dust* and the Black Independent Cinema Movement." In *Black American Cinema*, pp.118-144. Edited by Manthia Diawara. New York: Routledge.

Beckles, Hilary McD. 1989. *Natural Rebels: A Social History of Enslaved Black Women in Barbados*. New Brunswick: Rutgers U. P.

Busia, Abena P. B. 1988. "Words Whispered over Voids: A Context for Black Women's Rebellious Voices in the Novel of the African Diaspora." In *Black Feminist Criticism and Critical Theory*, pp.1-41. Edited by Joe Weixl Mann and Houston A. Baker. Greenwood: Penkeville.

Dash, Julie. 1992. "The Script: *Daughters of the Dust*." In *Daughters of the Dust: The Making of an African American Woman's Film*, pp.75-164. New York: The New Press.

"Dialogue between Bell Hooks and Julie Dash." 1992. In *Daughters of the Dust: The Making of an African American Woman's Film*, pp.27-67. New York: The New P. "Grace Nichols in Conversation with Maggie Butcher." 1988. *Wasafira* (Spring): 17-19.

Griffin, Gabriele. 1993. "'Writing the Body': Reading Joan Riley, Grace Nichols and Ntozake Shange." In *Black Women's Writing*, pp.19-42. Edited by Gina Wisker. New York: St. Martin's P.

Guerrero, Ed. 1993. *Framing Blackness: The African-American Image in Film*.

Philadelphia: Temple U. P.

Hamilton, Virginia. 1985. *The People Could Fly: American Black Folktales*. New York: Knopf.

Liddell, Janice. 1994. *Imani and the Flying Africans*. Trenton, New Jersey: Africa World P.

Marshall, Paule. 1983. *Praisesong for the Widow*. New York: Plume.

Morrison, Toni. 1977. *Song of Solomon*. New York: New American Library.

Nichols, Grace. 1983. *I is a Long Memoried Woman*. London: Karnak House.

"A Writer's Work with Toni Morrison." 1990. A World of Ideas with Bill Moyers, a videorecording (Part 1). PBS Video: Public Affairs Television, Inc. Produced and directed by Gail Pellett.